This beautiful devotional is like a whisper from God, straight into our hearts. It's for any of us who need reassurance that we're going to make it. Women will encounter God in a fresh way through these pages. These gentle words offer hope in hard times, peace in painful times, and a reminder of God's enduring love in lonely times.

Jennifer Dukes Lee, author of *Love Idol*

Loop is just beautiful—a rich, inviting collection of love letters from our Father in heaven to his daughters on earth. Jennifer's sensitive, wise voice makes *Loop* a joy to read.

Shauna Niequist, author of *Bread & Wine*

On the days I feel tired and worn down by how small my life feels, Jennifer's words about God's love for his daughter's? They always bring me home to who I am in Him. And it's a gift.

Lisa-Jo Baker, community manger of Dayspring and author of *Surprised by Motherhood*

Jennifer Camp's *Loop* is reminiscent of *Jesus Calling*. It beckons us into the heart of the Father, whispering love to the weary soul and breathing purpose to the wayward pilgrim. It's a devotional that ushers all of us home.

Emily T. Wierenga, award-winning journalist and author of *Atlas Girl*

Loop is like sitting down with a cup of coffee for your heart—it will refresh, energize, and inspire you.

>   **Holley Gerth, best-selling author of *You're Already Amazing***

Loop makes me feel like I'm sitting on my couch, wrapped up in a blanket, with a cup of tea, and the Father is right next to me, whispering sweet, tender words to my tired, sometimes-forgetful heart. You can't help but feel closer to God and be reminded how much you're loved.

>   **Elisabeth Klein, author of *Unraveling* and *At the Corner of Broken and Love***

'Twice a week and let it percolate?!' Never have I seen a devotional work begin on that note, never have I more needed one that does. These are deep and startling pages, just what our souls need.

>   **Nancy Ortberg, author of *Looking for God: An Unexpected Journey Through Tattoos, Tofu and Pronouns***

Jennifer Camp has created a refreshing and restorative gift with *Loop*. Jennifer's passion for stirring women's hearts to the truth of what God believes about us is thoughtful and lovely. A wonderful resource!

>   **Jenni Catron, church leader and author of *CLOUT: Discover and Unleash Your God-Given Influence***

Loop meets you in those moments when you desire to sit quietly with God but simply can't get your mind to settle. Within the pages of *Loop* rests an invitation to listen to the heart of God. Jennifer is simply the messenger, overflowing the wisdom she's gleaned from life lived at the foot of the Cross and steeped in Scripture. In her fearless pursuit of the presence of God, she discovered that stilling her soul was the beginning of hearing from Him. In *Loop,* she invites us to do the same, inspiring us to create a habit of listening to the still small voice of God in our everyday life.

Elisa Pulliam, author of *Impact My Life: Biblical Mentoring Simplified*

Loop is a giant exhale, an assurance you long for daily but weren't aware you needed. Each reading is a breath of confirmation. Jennifer's inspired words are a love letter sliding across your cluttered kitchen table, a surprise of being known by the Creator.

Shelly Miller, Writer and Blogger of Redemptions Beauty

Loop declutters for a few moments our messy, busy lives and invites us to prepare ourselves for God's voice. His loving, ever-responding voice. And that? That is what I need more of in my life. Space to listen to my God.

Jen Ferguson, author of *Clean Eyes, Pure Heart*

Sometimes we struggle to really drink deep the love and joy God has for his children. His loving words often glance off us, when they should be sinking in and transforming us. Jennifer draws out the precious promises of Scripture, helping us slow down and see the life-changing truth they contain. *Loop* will help you see the God who is close and who loves you so very much.

Kelly Givens, editor at Salem Web Network, iBelieve.com

Be blessed and changed and deeply encouraged as you read *Loop*.

Mary DeMuth, author of *Wall Around Your Heart* and *Everything*

Jennifer is extending her hand towards us as the reader. Her invitation will bring your deepest desires what they are truly longing for...abandoned love in Him!

Angela Toth, co-founder of Toth Ministries

I am so encouraged by the words Father God speaks to me through Loop. Jennifer's words have touched my heart so much and I am thankful for her faithfulness. She is amazing, her heart is amazing. She is such a blessing.

Nicky Cahill, Writer, Salt and Sparkle, TV Producer, BBC Worldwide

loop

what women need to know

Jennifer J. Camp

Gather Ministries

Los Altos, California

For His girls—

the women eager to hear.

And for Justin—

the mighty oak behind me,
encouraging me to stay close.

Contents

loop

contents

loop

contents

13

Introduction
I Have a Letter for You

LOOP BEGAN as scribbles in early hours when the house lay mostly still. It began as a plea, "God, can you tell me again how much you love me? Can you remind me again who I am?"

Loop also began in a heart that was lonely. It began in my search for deeper connection—relationship I couldn't find in the circles at church or even in the pages I would read, eagerly, about God.

Loop began in my realizing this fullness God promised was missing in my life. And I began to wonder if the solution was fairly simple: if God was an intimate God—Abba Father—who loved to communicate with His children, perhaps I simply needed to wake up to what He was longing to say to me. Perhaps I needed to attune my heart to what God was whispering to me, his daughter.

Of course, there was never time to pray and sit still, it seemed. Work and lists—and even relationships—pressed in. How could I find time to listen to God's voice speaking? There seemed always something to prove, something to do, something to check off the list that would never end.

Yet the pace of striving, of keeping up, exhausted me. Something had to change.

What Had to Change

I was tired of trying to find peace and joy on my own. I was tired of trying to feel okay, on my own. I was tired of striving to be good enough, on my own. So, finally, weary and desperate, I prayed in a new way. I decided to speak less to God and, rather, listen more.

When I prayed, I began to wait on God's response. I figured, if he loved me like he says he does in the Bible, he would want to be with me and speak to me. My prayers were now less of a list of requests and pleas. They were times of worship. I would think about God and wait on him, listening attentively. Eyes closed, pen in hand, I'd write down what I heard him whisper to my heart. Simply, I expected God to show up.

And this was the beginning of me saying yes to full life. This was the beginning of me abandoning the old attempts of creating an identity for myself and, rather, listening to God's whispers about who I really was. Listening to God's voice—desiring to hear Him and listen to his words to his daughters—is what *Loop* is all about.

What Loop Is

Loop is simply this: a collection of whispers to my heart as I asked God what He wants to say to His daughters. Daughters who are busy. Daughters who are weary. Daughters who are lost. Daughters who are finally ready to lay down their burdens. Daughters who are eager to abandon the lies they've been believing—about God, about themselves, about how they are made and what they are designed to do. Loop is written for you.

For God is a Father who wraps His arms around you. God is a Father who delights in telling you, this daughter he created, you are loved. God is a Savior who reaches out His hands to you and invites you to dance and run and laugh with Him in a secret place—a place of beauty and richness and safety and adventure you may have yet never seen. God is a Counselor who whispers reassurance and truth and encouragement and wisdom, reminding you who you are, how you are not alone, and how you are made to live.

What Loop is Not

Loop is not a replacement for reading Scripture; nor is it a replacement of Scripture. It is simply a nudge, a layering of love song, a note scrawled down and folded a half dozen times and passed to you across the kitchen table. Opened up, the note is an invitation to listen to God's whispers, not just with your head but with your heart. For *Loop* could not have been written down to begin with—for it would not have been heard—if the listener was not present with expectation and an open heart.

How to Read Loop

Here is the invitation for you. Read *Loop* in a quiet place, if you can. Or read it in the in-between moments, the minutes before work and/or after school drop off, the minutes when you go to the sink for a glass of water, or when you are about to do your turn walking the dog. Read it in the morning when you rise, or at night, right before you go to sleep. A place of stillness is best, as it is in that place you are most likely able to be attentive to the concerns of your own heart. However, anywhere will do—for God is going to speak to you any way he can.

Loop was initially shared as an email devotional to be read twice a week. And I still think reflecting on one *Loop* at a time, for a few days, before moving on to the next one, is a good way to go. No matter how or when you read *Loop*, though, I encourage you to listen carefully to the words. After all, this is a letter just for you. What is God speaking to your heart? Return to the entry throughout the week, as each time you read it, the words will have new meaning. Each *Loop* is going to be received by the listener in a different, and new, way every time. And that's the best.

Listening with you, sister,

Jennifer

Take a Step

And behold, I am with you always
— Matthew 28:20

I AM THE ONE who carries you through moments
when you feel you can no longer stand. I have
desired you, loved you, from the beginning. I would
not leave you. You are where I want to be. So, I
remain close. I remain with you.

What is it like to remain with Me?
Remaining with Me is not a stagnant place. We may
wait together, be wise and patient and take small
steps together. But when it is time to step forward

into something more, you must rely even more on my love for you to propel you on. But I am with you here, too.

I whisper, "Go on, girl, my daughter. Remember I am with you." You are ever invited deeper—deeper into the knowledge and awareness of my love for you.

Take a step with Me. Remember we go together.

Fresh Beginning

Therefore, if anyone is in Christ,
he is a new creation — 2 Corinthians 5:17

THE BEGINNING is such a good place to be, my
darling. There is much in store. But there is
acknowledgment of what came before the beginning
to mark this moment as a beginning. And in that
place I was there, too. But let's start where beginning
is—the union of Me and you, the awakening of your
heart, bit by bit, to Me. I awaken you further, now.

These first starts are for you to appreciate the
moments that came before them—to see where I was,

what I was doing, before you recognized my presence. Let me take you back to where I was when you couldn't see Me there. Perhaps the definitions of beginning will need to be rewritten. *I always begin again in you, child.*

I am the discovery of the beginning—all hope and life in you. I will give you a fresh start this day. I give you new breath, new eyes, new adventures to set out on with Me. But I want to start this beginning by going back to where I've always been with you.

I have always been with you, child, even when you couldn't see it. I want to show you now.

Planting

As each has received a gift,
use it to serve one another — 1 Peter 4:10

MY DARLING, let Me create something new within you today. I plant seeds of hope within you, and I promise to bring you joy.

Do you believe I can and I will? Truly, do you believe? Do you now ask what will it require, this planting? Do you wonder what you have to give to receive gifts of hope? May I ask you—is there somewhere else that you could receive these gifts, on your own?

You have a choice: receive the gifts—my gifts to you, my girl—or not. But you can't find hope on your own. And you can't find joy on your own.

Do you believe I can give these gifts to you? Do you believe I want to? Why worry about what the gifts will require of you to receive them?

It is your willingness to receive the gifts that make my cost of giving them to you worth it. I give them to you before you can receive them because I have made you, too.

You are a gift to my heart, my beloved daughter. I want to give you good gifts. Believe that I am for you, child, not against you.

The requirement of receiving hope and joy is trusting Me more than yourself, loving Me more than yourself. And I give you this gift, too, to be able to do that.

Do you open your heart to receive that gift, too?

Something More

For we know, [sisters] loved by God, that he has chosen you — 1 Thessalonians 1:4

MY DAUGHTER, I see you. So beautiful. Daughter, you are so beautiful.

I know you feel distracted by many things, but I call you to something greater. It is greater not because of the size of it or because it will give you security or fame.

It is greater because it gives you the joy of your heart, the heart that sings with Me and knows my name and the sound of my voice in you. It is greater because it is best for you. It is what I have made for you to do, with Me.

Remember that only the things that I call you to do with Me will bring you joy—the deep, true joy that makes you glad you are living and that give you energy and excitement to raise that weary head of yours to face another day.

The things I call you to do with Me may make you tired, your body growing weary from work and your heart aching from the love I give you for others. But your soul is not weary.

Your hope in Me and the joy you have in completing with Me the task I have given you to do spurs you on so that you can't imagine life before this joy. But you do remember, don't you?

You know what it feels like to be weary of spirit, weary of heart. Let Me take those burdens, child. Let Me take the weight of regret and indecision and worry. Let Me carry you and bring clarity to your days. Eyes on Me, child.

What I give you to do brings joy and challenge, hope and work. And it is work that stirs your heart and brings life to your days because then you are not distracted by other things and are working alongside Me.

I Do Not Leave

I saw the Lord always before me, for he is at my right hand — Acts 2:25

DAUGHTER, I pour my light into you. I guide you and do not leave you. I have good plans for your life. I love when you step toward Me to realize them.

There is discouragement along the way—and distraction, too. But I keep walking ahead, and I reach out my hand, and I do not forsake you. I do not abandon you.

The path is filled with rock that can cause you to stumble—and weeds that entangle and attempt to trip you up. But I clear the path, in the midst of difficulty and sometimes-rocky roads. *I clear the path.*

My voice in you, these whispers to your heart, my words a blade of truth that swipes away uncertainty and doubt. Walk in the way I've prepared for you, this way full of twists and turns and hills and valleys, deserts and lush mountain-scapes.

I've walked this path. I walk it with you. How could I leave you?

You were made for this—to be with Me, walking this path, the path we walk together. Faith is not knowing the details of what the future holds, but trusting Me to be with you in it.

So keep walking with Me, in faith, along the path I've prepared just for you. That is where you will cling to Me most tightly, where you will feel my gaze steadfast upon you, when I will hold you. *Daughter, I never let you go.*

I Come Again

He brought me out into a broad place; he
rescued me, because he delighted in me
— Psalm 18:19

HOLY DAUGHTER, stand and claim your place,
the one I've saved just for you. You are the rescued
one, the redeemed and beautiful one. Oh, how I
delight in you.

How I love to look on you and hold you.
How I love to show you where I am and rescue you
again. I have rescued you already, but I love to show
you how I rescue you again.

31

loop

I come again and again, for you. I can't get enough of you.

I have so much love for you it cannot be contained. I am unabashed in my joy and love for you. I hold nothing back. How can I hold anything back? It is not who I am. I cannot change who I am.

And, my daughter, how you delight Me. How I love to be with you; I sing songs of joy over you. I created the music of your heart—and to that, together, we dance. Let Me show you more of Me.

Let Me take you further in. There is so much more to show you. There is so much more—the two of us together, to see.

Not on Your Own

For it is you who light my lamp; the Lord my
God lightens my darkness — Psalm 18:28

I STAND WITH YOU, daughter. You are not out
there on your own. Pause and see Me. Look for Me.
Heed Me. Desire Me. I care less about what you do
than about your seeing and heeding Me.

Daughter, it feels so hard to trust another, to
need another, to let down your guard and be raw
and real and open. But what have you got to hide? I
live in you. Let that light shine.

Yes, you mess up and feel weak. Remember,
I did not design you to be strong on your own.

You are the lamp lit by Me. You are the beginning of hope for another as you model trusting in Me and feeling like you don't have what it takes on your own. *I do not ask you to go ahead, on your own.*

Cling to Me. I am steadfast. Cling to Me. I give you words. Cling to Me—a life of prayer, each thought and action in accordance with my spirit in you. *You are not alone. Do not separate from Me.*

You are mighty in my name and go boldly where I go. Boldness, on your own, is not boldness, but weakness and pride. Lay that down, my love. *I have more of Me to give you.*

Why I Rescue

He has delivered us from the domain of darkness and transferred us to the kingdom of his beloved Son — Colossians 1:13

MY DARLING, my delight, those birds that dance so high in the sky . . . I made. They sing and they swoop, and I rescue them when danger falls. *I rescue you, my darling.*

I rescue you from mediocrity, from hesitation, from doubt and stunted curiosity. Imagine Me, looking at you, before you, clearing the way to rescue, so that you can rescue. *I rescue you so that, with Me, you can rescue.*

I paid a price for you, and I would do it again. I would never stop rescuing. But I did it once, and it was complete. So that, yes, you can rescue now daughter.

I call you to imagine possibilities of hope so that now you can rescue. I carry my name within you—my heart beating in time with yours. Go forth into openness with Me. Bring forth those daughters and sons who don't know what rescue means.

I rescue you. Now go tell them.

I Give You True Gifts

I in them and you in me, that they may
become perfectly one — John 17:23

MY DAUGHTER, I am the way, the truth, and the
light. Whoever knows Me will not perish but have
eternal life. I am the gatherer, the one who comes
and brings hope and keeps you close to Me. You may
move away from Me, but I still remain. *Let nothing
separate us.*

There is freedom in laying down that restless
heart. Be steadfast, with Me. You have what it takes.
I have given you a heart that, in truth, desires Me
more than anything. This is how you are steadfast,

this is how you do not waver, this is how you stay close to Me: when your heart is filled with Me. *Desire more of Me.*

I give you the true things for which your heart desires. Truth, hope, joy, freedom—this is life with Me.

In the midst of trial, I give you these things. In the midst of heartache and trouble, I remove anxiety and worry, and I give you these things. In the midst of storms and busyness and patches of quiet when I feel not so near, I give you these gifts of your heart. Because I gather and restore what is mine. *I have designed you, and I know what you need.*

Let my love overflow on you. Let my gifts be easy to receive.

Where I Am

Not that we are sufficient in ourselves to claim anything as coming from us, but our sufficiency is from God — 2 Corinthians 3:5

I AM THE BEGINNING, my love. I am your beginning. There is nowhere else you need to look. There is nothing else you need to chase down. I speak to your heart—in whispers, in moments.

This moment now, my dear. This moment now. And the next one . . . and when you turn away from these printed words, too.

I do not exist on the page, but in your heart—in the moments I give you. Each breath a testament to my life in you. Each sigh and tear and reaching for Me. I am in the middle.

I am right here, in the middle, child. You are held, and I can't ever let you go. It is not about what you do. You do from life in Me and you strive in life without Me.

Reaching for Me is not the same as striving to attain something on your own. Reach for Me, and you have Me. Reach for other things—without Me—and these are things you should not attain. Let Me show you what is for us to do together.

The Light You Carry

Then shall your light break forth like the dawn, and your healing shall spring up speedily — Isaiah 58:8

DARKNESS, MY CHILD, is only temporary. The light inside you illuminates the darkness. You carry the lamp. I keep it lit. You bear within you the flame my breath of life ignites.

It is the light that guides your feet, that marks your path, that casts away shadows. You, my darling, are a light bearer—a truth teller. You mark the way of truth with the path you walk, in light. *Walk in my light, child.*

I produce the light, and I illuminate you. I make you shine. There is light within you that cannot be put out, and it spurs you on and guides my children home.

I keep it lit, for you to recognize my voice. I keep it lit, for you to trust Me more and know my goodness is not temporary. I keep it lit, that the world's darkness has a light to guide them. I keep it lit, so that when you stumble, you will not be afraid . . . for you will know the way home.

Respond to that light within you, my love. *You shine, with Me in you.* It is beautiful to behold.

Leading and Listening

The Lord your God who goes before
you will himself fight for you
— Deuteronomy 1:30

I LEAD, you follow. There is a time for leading—
following Me. And there is a time for listening,
trusting my voice in you and waiting on it. *Know that
I speak.*

Lead by listening, not on your own. Then
leading comes from the true place I call you to—the
foundation that you can never doubt, the rock that

43

never wavers, sure footing where you can always stand.

I ask you to go ahead, sometimes into new places, but they are places where I have been. And I show you the way to go there. You never head out—leading the way, on your own. *I am your guide, your beacon, your map, your voice.*

I am the one who goes ahead and marks the trail. Sit and listen first, so you can recognize my voice when you head out into new territory, the two of us, together.

Do you hear Me? Do you recognize Me? Do you know the feel of my arm around you, my whisper of hope and love? *I am your strength. Nothing else.*

I am the one who loves you and sends you out, with my voice in you. There is no place I won't speak.

To Bear Fruit

I am the vine; you are the branches. Whoever
abides in me and I in him, [s]he bears much
— John 15:5

I AM THE VINE OF LIFE. I bear fruit—the fruit of
my Father. My Spirit dwells in you that you may bear
my fruit, too. To bear fruit you trust the pruning and
grafting of branches by the Gardener.

To bear fruit you must trust—trust that good
will come, that you are cared for, my darling. *You are
so beautifully cared for.* Each drop of rain to quench
your thirst: my words in you guiding you to stay with
Me. Each gust of wind through your branches: fresh
air for your leaves.

I give you nourishment for your soul, a place to rest, a body to go with Me, a mind to drink of Me, a heart to be stirred with Me. I am the Vine of Life. I am strong and steady and the one on whom you depend.

You are my fruit, and in you I produce much fruit. Trust in my care and watch more beauty come—a fragrance that brings life and joy when breathed in.

Untangled

Other seeds fell on good soil and produced grain, some a hundredfold, some sixty, some thirty — Matthew 13:8

IN THE BREAK OF MORNING, as sunlight falls gently on flowers not yet opened, know that I fall softly, too. I am the light that covers all the land. Some flowers stretch their stems high to be covered by the light. Some are tangled in weeds that block the light from reaching their faces. And darkness is what covers. *But light filters through all darkness, child.*

There is no thing that cannot be untangled. There is a way out from the mess of secrets and distorted truths, from a focus on treasures that sap

47

energy from weary roots rather than let sweet water flow.

I reach down with my hands and untangle the mess—creating order from disorder. But all can get tangled again. *The light is above you. Stand tall. Rise to it. I show you where it is.*

Roots are thirsty. Let them drink and not be choked. You are cared for in your own place, with my hand tending you, my light touching you, my word quenching your thirst. To get untangled, you must focus on Me. You must stand straight and tall in my light, wanting it to touch you.

You must want Me to touch you. You must want Me to care for you. You must want Me to give you what you need and be willing to bear the adjustments of untangling.

In what are your roots tangled? How are your leaves too close to weeds that they wither from lack of sufficient light? Do you want Me to show you? Do you let Me untangle you? Do you want to stretch upwards, away from this mess I did not create for you to thrive in? *Will you let yourself be transferred and replanted in rich, fertile soil?*

Where Beauty Is

Arise, my love, my beautiful one, and come
away — Song of Solomon 2:13

I AM BEAUTY—in all its dimensions, in all ways
beauty is characterized. I am the foundation.

Beauty is distorted when my heart is not
heeded, when my heart in my children is silenced. I
hold my hand below the heavens. It sweeps color like
a brush—folding within the creation itself.

Beauty can be hidden between folds, in
cracks in hard hearts. Beauty exists in softening, in
ground fertile, expectant, wanting to be watered.
Beauty is possibility, the expectation of pushing

through the rough patches until there is ever greater softening. Hardness—a hard heart—is the opposite of beauty. *There is no becoming more beautiful.*

What I have created *is* beauty—the foundation of all I create is beauty. Beauty needs to be discovered. I see it. I see you. I see all possibility of love blooming in hard places. That blooming—that discovery—that claiming of the beauty that is you, is realizing the fullness of who you are. You, my girl, have beauty that cannot be ignored, cannot be buried under the ground. But it is, sometimes, isn't it?

May I peel back the layers to show you what I created? May I show you what, in you, I see?

Fear Fades

The Lord is my light and my salvation;
whom shall I fear? — Psalm 27:1

MY DARLING, I am in places of fear. I go there to chase it away, trample it with my foot. Heading into new territory with Me is a beginning to trust Me more deeply. It is a forgetfulness of self, a reliance on Me, a looking to Me for strength.

Fear can't stay when your eyes are on Me, when you seek Me. It must flee because you are willing to go where I go.

A softening occurs when a heart formerly full of fear relaxes and looks to Me. Focus on Me wipes it away. The situation causing the fear may still exist,

but there is hope now. There is truth now. There is
clarity.

You can only see clearly when you look to
Me—for strength, for understanding, for wisdom, for
courage. The mindset of fear focuses on the self. *Let
Me help you turn your heart to Me.*

Going out into unfamiliar territory—being
stretched, walking in faith, does not mean you are
alone. Fear should be most distant then. I am with
you. I go with you, there in the places I call you to. I
said it before: keep your eyes on Me, child. *My eyes
are on you.*

My Fragrance

For we are the aroma of Christ to God among
those who are being saved and among those
who are perishing — 2 Corinthians 2:15

I AM FOR YOU. I am with you. I go before,
knowing what is ahead. I stand behind, my hand on
your shoulder, so close you can smell my presence.

Yes, there is a fragrance of my Spirit. This is
where I invite you to live—your truest self, stripped of
all insecurities, all what-ifs, all doubts and fears and
pains.

Breathe deeply, my dear one. Breathe in
sweetness and hope. Breathe in newness and the
clean air I bring. *I draw you in.*

Let Me be your strength. There, you are glorious. Let Me be the hand you hold—all weight lifted, all sorrow behind. Let Me cup your face in my hands. Let Me look on you. Let Me hold you. Let Me walk next to you. Match my stride. *I show you how.*

There is a pace—within this fragrance of my presence—where I invite you to stay. Keep that pace. You know the pace, the rhythm, the movement of your moments when you can breathe Me and smell the fragrance of Me with you.

I envelop you. I carry you. And all whom you meet will be in my presence, with you, too. They will be enveloped in the fragrance of Me. All you do with Me points the people you meet to the fragrance. Let it spread. Keep in step. Check the pace. Let it be a rhythm that is natural.

Practice. Breathe. *I show you how.*

Heed the Rhythm Within You

In returning and rest you shall be saved; in quietness and in trust shall be your strength
— Isaiah 30:15

MY DARLING, I know the road feels long, that the pace seems fast, that the future feels so uncertain.

My darling, let's just start here: I see you. I know you. Can we just pause . . . for just a moment?

There is a rhythm to our days together—a rhythm within you that I ask you to not ignore. I am looking at you. Right here.

You are the one I have chosen. You are the one I dreamt of. From the beginning, when I made you, there has been a rhythm. There is a pace I set for you, a pace where you feel most at home.

Trust that. Trust that it can be discovered— trust that we do things together where you don't have to race to keep up. If you are racing, it is outside of the rhythm I have placed within your heart.

Trust my pace for you. Pause to find it so you can find it and walk into it: my whisper, to the right, to the left. I show the way, and I set the pace. *Deep breath, my love.*

My gaze is on you. Pause to see Me seeing you. That's the pace, a deep breath, a pause, a watching Me for the pace . . . And when you find Me, the pace becomes a part of you . . . and you see Me . . . and you see how I never turn away.

What it Means to Mother

Whoever does the will of my Father in heaven is my brother and sister and mother
— Matthew 12:50

MY LOVE, do you hear that music, the one where we dance and your steps are light and you swing?

You mother in the quiet places and in the moments when it is loud and it feels impossible to hear. You mother in the choices, the choices to love beyond yourself, the sacrifice that comes with friendship, the nurturing of an arm across a

shoulder, the carrying of beauty within you, the
permission for Me to care for you, to pour love into
your heart so that the ripple of my love continues.

A waterfall begins with a drop, and then a
cascade, a drifting through quiet places, a collection
until the drops pour past, all together. Mothering
happens in the combination of Me holding you in
my hands and letting my fingers open a bit to let you
pour out what I give. *You can only mother from what I
give.*

Mothering is a collection of hopes for the
future, a belief in good things and the willingness to
go to the hard places for those you love. It is the
shepherding of children, the gathering of
expectation for a future that is to come. *It is faith in
possibility for people beyond yourself.*

To mother is to press in and give out and
never give up. It is to hold on tight and let go, all at
once. It is to walk beside and listen close and not fall
away, even though the pain comes and it is hard to
stay. *To mother is to stay.*

And the staying isn't what you think it looks
like sometimes. It is the supporting of the one you
hold close while believing it isn't always you who
knows the way. *In mothering, without Me, you
don't know the way.*

To mother is to trust and laugh and cry and
wave good-bye. It is to come again, despite rejection.
It is to provide, when you feel you have nothing to

give. It is to look beyond yourself for strength and feel frail and helpless and fall and believe that you will be caught so that you can lift your knees and see what is before you, the Son.

Mothering is not just about bearing a child. It can be that but it is not just that. You mother through loving whom I bring your way. Come on, daughter, look whom I bring.

It's Just Not that Complicated

Choose this day whom you will serve . . . But as for me and my house, we will serve the Lord — Joshua 24:15

MY DARLING, I am here. I am the whisper in your heart that says stay, that says run. *Stay with Me . . . .Run for more of* Me. Sometimes I just await your desire to be with Me, for that desire within you for more of Me, to awaken. *Awaken, child.*

You want more of Me? You want to see Me? You want to be with Me? Yes? You do? It's just not complicated, child. With Me, life isn't complicated. Choices are not complicated. But choose.

I love that you can choose. It is hard to be abandoned, forgotten, ignored. It is hard to be shunned, rebelled against, spat upon. It is hard to be yelled at, rejected, blamed . . . but I want you to choose.

Be full of Me and be strong. Or reject Me and be weak. You can choose. Run to Me, or run away. Turn away and live on your own; do not truly live . . . Choices. Yes, choose.

And yes, choosing can break hearts. I know what it means to live with a broken heart, to feel the burden of choice, the weight of rejection and pain and wretchedness. I see it, face to face. And I do not turn away. *Choose.*

Choose, as it is too good—this life worth more than anything, more than any words can describe— to not choose. You receive life from choosing. You receive life from your decisions, the choices you make, on your own.

My heart is in you, yes. But I let you choose. And it is trusting that I am in you that helps you make the choice:

Choose Me. Choose love. Choose more. Desire more.

loop

I love you, my darling. This life I made for you.

I Love You

But I have this against you, that you have
abandoned the love you had at first
— Revelation 2:4

YOU ARE LOVED. You tell me, "I love you." And I
love you back.

You love from my first love, and I fold you
in. Your first love is what excites you about
beginning your day, what brings reassurance to your
heart, what brings a measured step and exhilaration,
too.

With first love you are steadfast and eager
and curious and expectant. Your heart wakes to

hope—hope of being together, hope that there will be time together. You desire, simply, to be with the one you love, side by side.

When you love, you see with open eyes and open heart the look in your loved one's eyes, the sound of their voice. When you love, you listen close for more. You are attentive and eager to absorb experiences—moments—with the one you love.

I know first love. But I know a heart of hesitancy, too. I know doubt—how you are made and what you are capable of and made to love.

That first love is your heart, my darling. Let's bring clarity to it. Let's figure out what it is.

Let me show you what you love first and what you are made to love first and if these two line up. There is only fullness with Me, my darling.

See Me Coming

Let me hear in the morning of your steadfast love, for in you I trust — Psalm 143:8

IN THE DISTANCE, I am coming. From afar, I walk towards you, my eyes always on you. I bend my ear close to you, your breath sweet on my cheek. You delight Me, my darling. *Want to run away together, just you and Me?*

Running away is staying—staying close—and going with Me. I delight when you stay. I have something for you—a plan, a task to do together. It is not what you think. It is what I reveal to your heart. *Trust your heart.*

When you see Me coming—in the distance coming for you—trust your heart. When I am near, when I am so close you know my presence in you, trust your heart.

Trusting means surrendering your will to mine. It means believing Me more than yourself. *I am in you.*

Trusting is recognizing my whispers and not your own without Me. Listen to the whispers to your heart when we are together.

Trust Me: I delight in you. I love to be with you. I guide the path for your heart.

Where Your Safety Is

The name of the Lord is a strong tower; the righteous . . . runs into it and is safe
— Proverbs 18:10

MY DAUGHTER, do not run away. Do not run from my presence. Here, here, my love, is where your safety is. Here, here, my love, is where your fast beating heart will slow. Here, here, my love, is where you are captured, fully captured by my love and free, all at once.

67

loop

My love, turn your face to mine. I take my hands underneath your chin and raise your eyes to meet mine. *Look.* Don't close your eyes or look down. *Look into my eyes, child.*

My child, my daughter, listen now. I have you. Let this penetrate your heart. I have you. Do not run away. You are the one I want. You are the daughter I made whom I formed with my own two hands.

My eyes are on you, child. They are always on you. And they are eyes of love, not condemnation. They are eyes soft and bold and sure in my love for you. *You are stunning, and I am captivated.*

You are perfectly made, and I delight in you. You are radiant, and I pour myself into you. You are my own, my girl, my daughter, my true one, my found one, my cherished one. I will never tire of being with you, holding you, wrapping you up in my arms.

Stay here, my love. *I stay.*

I Like to Be Where You Are

He said to them, 'Come and you will see.' So they came and saw where he was staying, and they stayed with him that day
— John 1:39

MY DAUGHTER, when I came to dwell with you, it was before you ever knew. But I have known you and sought you out and loved being with you.

Do you know I love to sit with you? Do you know I love to study your face? This face I touched and touch, now, even still?

69

I like to be where you are. As I am with you, do you know I invite you in, to be with Me, to stay with Me? Do you feel Me next to you?

There is a difference between feeling I am close and knowing I am in you. For I am in you, my love—and I invite you in, even deeper, still.

I say, "Come and see." Come with Me. See where I am. Stay with Me. Be with Me. Watch Me. Follow Me. Be close. Ask Me questions. *Come and see. I turn and answer.*

Be curious about what we do together. I love to hear your heart speak. I hear you. I delight in hearing you. Do not fear about the next turn in the road as we walk, as you follow. *Stay close.*

See the steps and the focus on what is ahead, all the while staying close to Me. Oh, my girl, I am close. *Come closer.*

I invite you in. Stay with Me awhile. I have so many things to speak to your heart.

I've Got You

Even there your hand shall lead me, and your right hand shall hold me — Psalm 139:10

YOU LOOK FOR ME, daughter. But you don't need to look far.

Oh, trust Me. Trust Me: when I say I am with you, nothing can separate you from my love. This is true. *Come deeper.*

Drink of these roots that do more than sustain. Yes, they hold you up. Yes, they let you reach high, to a new place, with Me. Yes, they give you courage, knowing you are held, knowing you will not topple. The stream that nourishes you will never run dry.

You do not do the planting in the best soil. That is for Me to do. You do not decide the weather—whether the sun will shine or rain will fall. You do not know when storms will bend your branches, the wind whipping off your leaves. You do not know when a branch will need to be cut, a root adjusted, fertilizer poured in and mixed with rich soil.

I am the one who cares for you, my love. I am the one who bends low, my hand upon you, my breath the sweet aroma of your soul.

Come, child. I take your concerns. I've got you. *I've got you.* I see you and care for you. You are growing. *You are becoming more and more yourself.*

Oh, how I love to tend to you and be with you! You are the one for whom I bend low and you see Me. *I am so close.*

The Definition
of Success

So as to walk in a manner worthy of the Lord,
fully pleasing to him, bearing fruit in every
good work and increasing in the knowledge
of God— Colossians 1:10

DAUGHTER, LISTEN. Trust your heart. What if
you believed you were enough? What if you believed
you were loved? Would you dance? Would you be
free?

My daughter, I am here. *I am here.* Lift up
your head. Lift up your eyes.

Do you care more about what others think than about following Me? Do not try to please the world, my love. It does not bring you joy. Being present, with Me, brings you joy.

Do not judge success. What is success? Who is qualified to measure it?

Is it full of my love? Does it represent Me? Does it bring a lightness of heart, a stirring towards truth? Does it call forth hope? Does it elicit freedom from the ties to this world?

Does it celebrate beauty? Does it make people free? Does it reflect my Son and His sacrifice? Does it foster obedience and a desire—bigger than one's self, for good?

Does it lay down striving? Does it suggest I am enough and all efforts to achieve joy and success on one's own is fruitless? Does it bring forth my fruit—patience, kindness, gentleness, love, mercy, thankfulness, tenderness, compassion, hope?

Does it prompt the laying down of selfishness? Does it unite my children and bring forth peace and unity? Does it represent Me? What is success? Oh, daughter, lay it down.

I am yours. I am the only success. I am the only way. I am the only life. I am the only life-giving work for you.

74

The Way to Wide Open Space

And let the peace of Christ rule in your hearts, to which indeed you were called in one body. And be thankful — 1 Colossians 3:15

MY LOVE, you know how I love to tell you, "Breathe deep"? You know how I love to quiet you, remind you I am here?

What does it look like? What does it look like to have peace in your heart?

Picture open space and beauty and the sounds of life. There may be a breeze blowing. You may feel it on your skin. Or you see the space within you. *It is open space within you where I enter in.*

Open space is opportunity. It is freedom. It is love. It is untamed obedience and desire and glory–Me in you spread out wide and deep and long.

I want more open space for you, my girl. I want more richness and abandonment of rules for the sake of following Me. *I know the way to open space.*

You may feel trapped right now, the world closed in and the list of obligations so long. But I come to you there, my hand extended. *See Me looking at you.*

In this place where there seems no place to turn, I invite you into open space. Wide open for you and Me to walk in wild, love-filled abandon together.

Where Your Story Begins

For you formed my inward parts; you knitted
me together in my mother's womb
— Psalm 139:13

DAUGHTER, YOU HEAR Me say it true: I begin a
new thing in you. The past is behind you. I was there
with you. I can show you where I was.

Looking back is not bad, but staying there is
not my plan. Let Me place my hand on the places of
pain, where you feel alone, where you cry out for
rescue.

loop

I have rescued you, daughter. I created your frame, the contours of your skin, the timing of the way your eyes close, just so. I know your makeup, all the details of you, your entire story. *I author you, daughter.*

The drafting of your story, your hand in mine . . . there is paper not more beautiful–curls of letters that make Me smile.

Daughter, the story of your name is written in my book, your beginning, the moment where you felt you ended and I begin. That is your beginning, child. *You begin where you end and I begin.*

And the story keeps writing, child. After beginning there is adventure. After beginning there is trust and falling and catching and believing and choosing and waiting. There is much waiting and beginning again. Your story running right off the page with Me.

The Treasure in Waiting and Listening

He who dwells in the shelter of the Most High
will abide in the shadow of the Almighty
— Psalm 91:1

WAIT IN THE SPACE where I am. Wait in
expectation, listening with your mind clear, alert,
open to all possibilities. Wait on Me.

My voice is in you. You hear the whisper of Me in the light, when fear is surrendered and I am your strength.

You hear Me in stillness—but stillness amidst clamor, too. But I quiet clamor within you. I still the storm and whisper, "I am here, my love. Keep your eyes on Me." *Take that deep breath now. Slowly now.*

Slow your pace, for just a moment. Stay in the stillness—retreat to quiet, where my voice is what you seek. Become conditioned to it, accustomed to moments of silence and openness and listening. *I create space within you, my darling.*

You feel stretched and overwhelmed and tired and unsure, and I show you the wide-open space within you, the place where I am. It is a place of comfort, of safety, of quiet, of companionship.

When you feel alone, head into that open space within you, with Me, and you will hear my voice within you, stirring you, whispering wisdom and love—guiding you deeper Home.

What It's Time for You to Do

Put off your old self, which belongs to your former manner of life and is corrupt through deceitful desires — Ephesians 4:22

MY DAUGHTER, hear the song in your heart for Me. Hear the song of longing, of beauty, of self-forgetfulness, for the sake of joy. *Surrender and receive more joy.*

What is it you need to surrender? What is it you need to believe more deeply about Me? What is it, child? *Oh, come, be rescued.*

Oh, come, hear the thunder in the distance, the rolling of the beat, my own heart speaking your name. Lay down, my girl. Lay down the future. *I've got you.* Lay down the past. *I've got you.*

Believe I am for you, that I come for your heart in ways you don't yet even know. But you want to know, don't you?

You want to see Me coming for you, running, my arms spread open. Daughter, turn it over again, that place in your heart that I touch, that I reach in and grasp and show you what it is you need to lay down. *Lay yourself down, my love.*

It won't hurt too much. I promise. And what is pain? Come—come deeper now. *Lay down. Come closer.*

It is only painful when the old self dies. Let it die again. Oh, the thunder rolls. My heart beating still. Let that self be killed to receive more of Me. I promise—it's worth any temporary pain.

Different
Expectations

And I heard the voice of the Lord saying,
'Whom shall I send, and who will go for us?'
Then I said, 'Here I am! Send me'— Isaiah 6:8

I AM HERE, even when you are tired. I am here,
even when you think I'm not. I am here, not
dependent upon your mood or your efforts. I am
separate from circumstances, but in the middle of all
moments, too.

Look for Me. Expect Me. Desire Me. Attune your heart to my voice.

Believe I speak words of love to you. Believe I love to be with you—whether it feels like I am close or not.

How would it look to live believing I am close, even when you can't see and hear and feel Me?

What does it mean to feel and hear and know Me? What are you looking for? What are you expecting?

What if you got rid of expectations of what it looks like to walk with Me and still knew I am with you? Isn't my life in you unique to my presence with all others? Isn't the making of you—your personality, your ideas and experiences so far, going to shape how you hear and see and experience Me?

How fun this will be! You expecting to see Me, be with Me . . . Because here's the difference, here is what matters: Know I am with you. Know I love you. Know I love to be with you. Won't you see Me and hear Me more then?

I do not change, but I tune your heart. I want you to know even these words are true.

When I Whisper to You

As for you, O Lord, you will not restrain your mercy from me; your steadfast love and your faithfulness will ever preserve me!
— Psalm 40:11

DAUGHTER, I KNOW. *I know.* It is not I who whispers, "You are alone." It is not I who whispers, "No one sees you, cares about you, loves you." Daughter, I do not delight to see you in pain, to see you suffering. Your heart cries out, in its weariness, in its grief, and oh, child, I pick it up. *I lift you up, child.*

I do not leave you sitting there, hopeless. I do not leave you there crying in an empty room. I fill the space in your heart that feels like breaking. I do repair work (my favorite kind), on you.

I know you want circumstances to change. I know you are frustrated and impatient—after all, you have been waiting so long . . . But my plan is not to bring suffering. If there is pain in a moment, in a situation, know, child, I can break through and be a beacon in the midst of it all.

I whisper . . . Come, my delight, lay all your troubles on Me. Come, darling, your hand belongs in mine, guiding you forward, moving you past sadness and through these walls into the new place I've created for you, a place where my light shines in the midst of dark, where my voice quiets all other whispers, where my gaze upon you buoys you up, teaches you how to stand again, reflects back your smile. *Smile, now, child.*

Rise for the joy that is yours to receive. Be surprised by the abundance of joy I have to give you.

I do not hold out on you. I do not leave you. I do not turn from you. I know your troubles. I hear your prayers. I know your desires and pleas. Oh, girl, I've got you. I know you.

Trust me now. Trust how I am here.

When You Need to Return

And standing behind him at his feet, weeping, she began to wet his feet with her tears and wiped them with the hair of her head and kissed his feet and anointed them with the ointment — Luke 7:38

MY DAUGHTER, you return with what you have. You lay yourself down, all of you, emptied. Because here, girl, in that posture, I make you clean.

    You return to be cleansed, to be renewed. You make the choice to come back to a place where you were before. But to return to Me—you are not going back to the same place because I have made you new. I have turned you around. I have touched your face with my hand, my other hand on your heart. *And girl, you are not who you were before.*

So returning is beginning, not going back. Returning is breathing fresh air into stale, unused lungs. Returning is marking the place where I was and claiming the new heart I've given you. Returning is bending; it is kneeling; it is spreading yourself out, waiting to receive.

In returning, your new eyes I give you show you the past with hope in the pain, light in the darkness, the little-girl-made-woman I have always loved and come to redeem again.

Stay here now, daughter, my adored one. I carry you now. I lift your head now. I let you bow low to be lifted high with new life. Believe returning is a re-turning—a reorienting, a readjusting, a revisualizing, a renewing. It is the revising of a story I've always seen, with a beginning and an end all the same. *New.*

Return with Me, darling. Return to Me now.

Turning

Peace I leave with you; my peace I give to you. Not as the world gives do I give to you. Let not your hearts be troubled, neither let them be afraid — John 14:27

YOU ARE MADE to remember Me . . . and forget Me, too. I gave you a mind to think and be influenced by many things. You hear this and feel that. What you read and see and hear—the experiences you have in this world—shape you, influence how you view the world and how you choose to live in it.

Your heart, too, is unique in how it is not wired to love Me, like a machine obeys a command. A machine does not feel. The heart I give you can love many things. And yes, you can forget Me, get distracted by this world and pull away from Me, stop loving Me. And yes, it breaks my heart—and angers Me, too.

I both pursue you and surrender you when I made you. I knew you would come to know Me, follow Me. But I knew you would be pulled away from Me, too. And this is why I keep pulling you back.

Right here, right now, you are pursuing Me. You lean in and listen and seek and desire more than what is physically seen in this world. *Go deeper, child.*

I chase you, and you can run away. But you can chase Me, too, and I will never turn away from you. I woo you. I desire you. But girl, when you forget Me, I don't stop desiring you. I don't stop loving you. I do not do as the world does. I am not fickle and impatient. I am not distracted. *I know whom I love.*

You are here, now, not forgetting Me. You are here, now, letting yourself be pursued. You are here, now, surrendering . . . aren't you?

Let me purify your heart so you know what you pursue and why you do it. Let Me woo you with kindness and love so your head is cleared and your heart knows what love is.

I come from a pure place, knowing every piece of you. Just turn, a little bit, towards Me. *I will help you turn even more.*

I Know What You Love

Arise, shine, for your light has come, and the glory of the Lord has risen upon you
— Isaiah 60:1

OH, DAUGHTER, what do you love? I know what it is, you know. *I know what it is you love.*

There is a daughter who lifts her hands and wonders if I see her. There is a daughter who feels reckless with her heart, who is not sure if it is what she can trust. There is a girl who is afraid to call Me "Home".

One day you will be gathered. One day what you love will be made even more clear. One day all hands will be joined—not one hand forgotten. All hands raised. All voices lifted. All hearts opened. All souls rescued. *Oh, girl, I rescue.*

There will be praising and your glory will shine. Daughter, I know what you love. Ask Me. Search Me. Listen to Me. Your name is written—your character formed yet continuing to be made new.

Oh, My Delight, the daughter I rescue, let Me show you more of Me. Let Me show you where I am and how I speak to you. Let Me grasp your hand. See Me beholding you. I show you what you love.

And then, daughter, do those things you love with Me. What I've given for you to love is my heart in you. Try it out. See more of Me. Hear Me more. Watch Me move in you. Come on now. I've got you. *I've got you.*

Rescued One, you are redeemed. Beautiful One, you shine so brightly, with Me. You are here, here with Me. I gather you. I am for you.

You are my desire.

Moment by Moment

Then you will call upon me and come and
pray to me, and I will hear you
— Jeremiah 29:12

MY LOVELY ONE, how wonderful it is to be with
you. Transitions are hard, aren't they? Trying to keep
up—one moment to the next. Going this way and
that way. I know your story. I know what's ahead.
How often do you think about that—that I know
what's ahead?

This moment . . . Now, this moment . . . Oh,
girl, stay.

Where does worry get you? How does it help? It hurts my heart to see how you strive, how you work so hard on your own. *Daughter, do nothing on your own.*

Confess it now. Lay down all the times you walked your own way without Me. Lay burdens down now—the ones you didn't even know you were carrying.

Daughter, you are made to move freely, without burdens. No matter what this moment holds, or the next one, I lighten your load. I am the steadfast one, the one who does not turn. I go forward into the moments ahead, preparing the way. Now walk in the way prepared for you. *Look for Me and find Me.*

Do not bow low that weary head. Look up. Look up at Me. Look at Me. I am here, delighting in you. I hold these moments, more precious than any jewel.

Let me show you how to perceive a moment with Me. Let me show you what freedom looks like, feels like, sounds like. This is all you have to do: Participate in the moments with Me. Experience life with Me.

Dance through now, child. A solid walking through hardship and uncertainty and love and freedom and my grace. Oh, how I give you myself— love and hope and grace. *You are not alone. Oh, no, never alone.*

loop

This moment, and this moment . . . This moment, remember, I spend with you.

What Worship Is

God is spirit, and those who worship him
must worship in spirit and truth — John 4:24

INTO THE DARKNESS where I am not afraid to go,
I will come. I will find you. You think you do the
things you do in secret, that no one notices or cares.
But I see you, and am with you. I do not depart. I do
not leave your side.

      With Me with you, always with you, how do
you worship Me? How do you choose to see Me,
recognize Me, adjust the eyes of your heart to know
where I am, with you?

My daughter, I turn your heart to Me, but you get to choose how I turn it, whether or not to acknowledge my presence in you. *Don't turn away, my love.*

Breathe in and know Me, daughter. Breathe out and know I've made you. Worshipping Me means listening and believing, in the moment, I am here . . . and letting Me help you see my face.

I have so much to show you. Just let Me show you all the places I am. In your work, in your home, in your relationships, in your dreams, in your personality . . . your actions, your frame, your voice, the curve of your chin and your jaw, the delight in your eyes. Yes, it is there. *I give you delight in your eyes, your heart for Me.*

You don't have to work so hard to chase anything down. Chase Me down and try to abandon all the things you wish would change.

Worship Me and all things look different. Worship Me with truth, for the renewed heart I give you, all fresh and clean and beautiful. And from that place of freedom and joy and new perspective, the journey with Me begins. *Let it begin, child.*

When You Wonder

Set me as a seal upon your heart, as a seal upon your arm, for love is strong as death, jealousy is fierce as the grave. Its flashes are flashes of fire, the very flame of the Lord
— Song of Solomon 8:6

MY GIRL, deep breath now. First of all, let Me tell you something: you don't have to have this life all figured out to live it well. You can keep going, one day at a time, looking for Me, not looking for Me . . . Your actions show Me what you love. I know your heart already. And your actions can move your heart to respond to Me in ways you can't, at the time, see.

Be encouraged: the moments of the going and the doing and the waiting and the longing . . . Couldn't they be responses to my whispers in you? You worry that you will miss Me. You look back on your day and you wonder, "Was that enough? Was I present with You, Father? Is working and wondering and running here and there a way to be with You? Is this the life You planned for me? Am I doing this right?" *Oh, girl, you don't disappoint Me.*

My daughter, I could not love you more, no matter what you do. Can you imagine living from that place, of knowing I adore you? Can you imagine awakening in the morning and knowing, no matter what is in store, you are not alone? My lovely one, I smile on you. I have to catch my breath when I think about you. *You captivate Me.*

Daughter, remember you are rescued. Remember, you are free. Remember, you are white as snow; cast all cares upon Me. Remember I am your strength. Remember I am the rock who will always help you stand. Remember, I came, and I know weariness and temptation. I know pain and frustration. I know hunger and thirst and the pressures of eyes of this world. I went before. I carry you now.

Going forward (steady now) . . . I am with you. No need to question where I am or if I love you or if you are doing a thing right. Your knowing my love for you is your guide.

My love, believe. That is how you measure a day.

Go Forward, Girl

I am the vine; you are the branches. Whoever abides in me and I in him, he it is that bears much fruit, for apart from me you can do nothing — John 15:5

LEAN BACK, now. I've got you. I circle my arms around you. I know what this day holds. A few twists and turns. A disappointment. A moment of beauty. A caress of your heart. (Yes, that's Me.) I hold your heart.

Do you want your love for Me to grow? Do you want to live fearlessly, completely, surrounded by

Me, with Me? Can you go ahead into new territory knowing you are not alone? Can your feet find the steps, your lungs the fresh air, your heart the pace I set? *I am with you.*

You say yes to where I call you and, of course, I am in it with you. *You do not go alone.*

The only risk, then, is not trusting Me, not believing in my sovereignty, my arms around you, my whisper in your ear. (It is the ear of your heart, my dear.)

Go. Go forward, not back. Go. Do not stay in the old place. I am always creating newness, removing the old roots and pruning branches so that new growth sprouts and green shoots see the sun.

There is always blooming planned. Never stagnation. Never stunted growth. Never dried up soil and neglected branches withering alone. Oh, girl, you will bloom and your glory will shine and you will see my face. And now, with my arms around you, you are set to bloom.

Here, with Me, wherever you go, in all the ways you say yes and let my tending to you occur, the blooming is taking place—and there is only more blooming to come.

I give you what you need, my daughter. Say yes, not no. Go forward, not back. Let your roots in Me deepen, and I pull you, in all your possibility, forth.

A Story Yours to Tell

And God saw everything that he had made,
and behold, it was very good. And there was
evening and there was morning, the sixth day
— Genesis 1:31

DAUGHTER, where do you run? How do you
doubt? What do you see when you look for Me?

Oh, girl, it's not silence. No, it's not empty
space. No, it's not memory failing. No, you don't
need to be smarter, quicker, a better listener. Maybe,
you could be more *you?*

Please don't run away from the girl I've made, hand-stamped with beauty, with talent, with a way to see Me and hear me unlike anyone else.

When I wrote your story, your beginning made me smile. You captured Me in how the details of your story were crafted. *You were held far before you were born.*

Your story gives life with my voice. I know there are things you'd like to forget, details you wish weren't part of your story. But the story is still beautiful, girl.

So, listen, how might we, together, look at your story through my eyes? I speak, and light appears. My hands crafted your frame. My breath is your breathing in and out. Let Me show you beginning again, and how the jagged points when you feel your heart breaking are places where you can be made even more beautiful and strong, the pruned branch grafted onto the vine. *I've never lost you.*

You have always been in my sight, your story on my lips and the story yours to tell. To whom can you tell your story? Whom do I bring to you? Who needs to know what it means to breathe the beginning, breathe the story of Life?

It's Okay to Be Uncomfortable

There is no fear in love, but perfect love casts out fear. For fear has to do with punishment, and whoever fears has not been perfected in love — 1 John 4:18

MY DARLING, I am not in the fear. I am in a new place, a separate place outside of it. *Step away, with Me.*

There is refreshment here. A new place to stand. There is room to move, to breathe, to spread your arms wide, hands open, fingers stretched, head relaxed.

I have work for you to do with Me, yes. We will go and I will push you to lean on Me and trust Me and do things uncomfortable for you to do alone. *But you don't go alone, my dear.*

And when you are with Me in the place that could feel so uncomfortable and stress-filled, on your own—when you depend on your own strength, when you look to yourself for answers—you can rest and relax in my presence. You can head out into new territory with Me and not feel scared.

Sometimes I don't tell you why it is I've asked for you to go to a place with Me. And that can feel uncomfortable, too. I know how you like answers.

But don't not go to this new place with Me because fear grabs hold of your heart. Don't let fear paralyze this girl-amazing-woman whom I love and adore so that fear is more powerful than this truth: I am here with you, holding your hand, not leaving your side.

I am enough. My presence is enough. Where I take you is enough. You are free here, in this place with Me, outside of fear and no longer trapped.

Stand up straight, girl. *Stand up.* You are not made to cower and fret and wring your hands. You are made to walk with eyes up, head held high, so you can see the path I take you. Together we go, just one step at a time, and into territory that may be

loop

unknown but will be safe and familiar too . . .
because I will be there. *And I am your home.*

Stop Second-Guessing

Now to him who is able to keep you from
stumbling and to present you blameless
before the presence of his glory with great
joy — Jude: 1 :24

MY DAUGHTER, you have not lost your way. You
have not missed out on a talent. You have not been
short-changed on intelligence, on beauty, on
personality, on gifts. You are not supposed to be
more coordinated, more funny, more organized,

more entertaining. You are not supposed to talk more, lead more, run more, do more.

You are not failing. You are not falling. You are not disappointing . . . Not when you are resting in Me. Not when you are looking to Me for your worth. Not when you are stopping to listen . . . and listening often enough so you recognize the sound of my voice.

Each daughter hears my voice differently, you know. But I am familiar, the same voice, recognized by the children who listen close.

My daughter, do not fret about being more or being less, doing the right thing and not making mistakes.

Take a risk and fall down. Take a risk and not know what you're doing. Take a risk and feel ill-equipped to finish the task. Take a risk and feel overwhelmed. And then stop . . .

Did you invite Me in? Did you do these things on your own, on your own strength? What strength was that, child?

You are made to soar, to risk—with Me—and see Me and grab my hand and live unlike you've ever lived before: Free.

Stop pondering the ways you need to do life differently. Stop second-guessing where I am and what I love doing with you and how amazing and beautiful I've made you to be.

You, my daughter, are the princess-warrior who knows who she is and goes forward saying yes to situations where you have to rely on Me.

And then, girl, you will see more of what I see. Then, girl, you will see more of *you*. And you will stop second-guessing. And life with Me will make more sense.

Do You Think I Love This World?

Yet a little while and the world will see me no more, but you will see me. Because I live, you also will live — John 14:19

MY DAUGHTER, look now. Look at Me. Raise your head again. I come for you.

What do you want to ask Me? Can I tell you the desire of your heart? I know you tire of staying in the same place. I know you are tired of looking at this world—but oh, how I love it. *Can I tell you how much I love this world?*

I love each bit of it. The cracks in the sidewalk, the pebbles mixed in desert sand. This is the landscape through which I walk. I walk where I want you to see. I walk through villages and down crowded streets. I sit at wells and wait, and I walk up mountains and sit on hills next to quiet seas.

I see beneath the facades, the walls my children build. I enter in with permission, and I long to make my home. I keep walking and knocking and waiting and listening. I know my home. I know my Father. I am Spirit who moves in you and wants to stay. And when you let Me in, and I stay, I remove the walls. I let you see beyond this world to what exists in it to save it.

I have come to save the world, and there are children who still do not know. They don't know there is a dream beyond food for their stomachs and a place to lay their head when they tire. *I am Home without walls.*

I am Home so you can rest here and see more of the things I see. Someday you will understand. You will see more. I give you glimpses, and I let your heart imagine the possibilities of true freedom, true love, true joy, true rescue. Oh, the day I come again! But you don't have to wait to receive my Spirit. And when you receive it, I equip you to paint the landscape anew for children who don't yet know Me in their hearts. *Oh, daughter, I love the world.*

I love these children. I love you. I come to rescue. I come to save. I come to love. I come to liberate children who are trapped and see no way of escape.

I come. Open your heart. I come. Look in my eyes. I come. I am all you need, and I go ahead.

Let me give you new eyes, a new heart—fresh courage and faith so my loved ones, the world, whom don't yet see Me can see Me in you. *Yes, let them see Me in you.*

And I will come to them, and they will know they are rescued and not forgotten, too.

What Your Heart Knows

And he is before all things, and in him all things hold together — Colossians 1:17

OH, DARLING, I know you want to touch Me—to reach out your hands and feel Me tangibly. Might I feel more real, then? Might I be more easily recognized? Look again. *Look again.*

Where is your restless heart? To what does it turn, if not to Me?

What can you see more tangibly that
distracts you from Me, when all my creation calls out
my name? What calls out something else? What does
not cry out holy? What does not cry out these words:
I have you. I want you. I rescue you. I redeem you. I
claim you. I made you. I beautify you. I hung on a
cross for you and faced death and won? *What tears
you away?*

From what do you get your self-worth? How
do you decide the value of a day? How do you choose
what is yours to do? What is your rhythm? How do
you receive energy? How do you find rest? *Oh,
daughter, where do I fit in?*

My daughter, I did not come to play second.
I did not come to trick you, con you into loving Me.
You only know who you are and what you're worth
through my love for you—my dying for you on the
cross. I would do it again for you. I would, you
know. But here's the thing: I did. *I did.* For you.

I do not ask you to love Me out of guilt, out
of obligation. I give you a heart that knows its way to
Me. It knows its true self. It knows its name. It
knows its place. It knows by whom it was made. It
knows the giver of all good things and how things
began and how ending isn't an option until the time
is finished here.

I say 'it is finished', and the beginning began
again. I called 'Father, I commit my Spirit to thee',
and that Spirit is now yours. And your heart knows

my Spirit. You know Me. My children know their name.

So touch these scars. Touch these hands. Let these fingers wrap around yours. My Holy Spirit—Me in you—holds on tight.

So, come on now, sweet one, you hold on tight, too. We've got things to do together.

The Way Time is Holy

That which is born of the flesh is flesh, and
that which is born of the Spirit is spirit
— John 3:6

YOU WANT TO KNOW what it looks like to pray
to Me? To be with Me? To listen to Me? You are full
of questions . . . when you pause . . . when you
ponder your heart. Questions about Me, about how
to live this day, about how to have more joy and
freedom . . .

Don't feel guilty about the hard days, the long days, the stumbles, even the falls. You could look back on them, analyzing them, thinking about how you could have done things differently and how tomorrow, no matter what (oh, you are resolute!) you will not repeat what you did before . . . Except, you fear you will.

You fear time passing so quickly—so quickly—and not being able to hold on tightly enough to time. A moment isn't holy in-and-of itself. It is Me, inhabiting the moment, which makes time holy. So how could you mess it up? How could you make a moment less holy? *Don't regret, child.*

The only purpose in *looking back* on time—in endeavoring to appreciate it—is *looking forward*, looking to where I was, in the moment, then. Look back, if you must, but only so you may see Me in the moment.

Oh, girl, I am in all things. I am in all moments. I cannot be quantified. Can how much I am with you be measured? Must you try to measure it? Must you try to measure Me?

You are the girl I held in the beginning and the girl I hold now, still. Your maturing is Me birthing you, again. I let you go, and I hold you, and I wait for you, and I pursue you. And we breathe, together: In. Out.

Time passing cannot measure my love for you—the increments growing or shrinking as you age. I birth you and you birth too—breathing in sync with my breath—becoming more and more what I see in you, all along.

Be born again, this day, with Me, becoming even more yourself: the girl I hold. Pause and drink now. Ingest Me more . . . this blood poured out, this body broken.

Be birthed again. (Eat and drink and be satisfied.) Only then will time be holy—celebrated, appreciated, not feared.

It's Not Too Late for You

Yet I will rejoice in the Lord; I will take joy in
the God of my salvation — Habakkuk 3:18

DAUGHTER, my spirit whispers, and some hear
more clearly than others. Some want to hear it . .
. and do . . . but mistake my words for something
else. There is a gift I give . . . to know, with certainty,
my words pressed upon a daughter's heart. And
there are some daughters who, of course, could hear,

because they know Me. But so many obstacles stay stacked in the way to discerning Me clearly.

Now, the ones who can hear—and listen intently—will not be disappointed. While they may not hear what they want to hear, they will not be disappointed because I do not disappoint. My presence, my true presence, does not disappoint.

This world brings with it much sadness, and my words get twisted and muddled. Purity becomes tainted. Translation is distorted. And I let my daughters act on the distorted messages. But I keep whispering truth their hearts—the hearts I created with my own breath—understand.

There is always hope in Me. There is always new life for you, my daughter, in Me. There is no daughter, despite her past, despite her mistakes, despite how she turns away, that could disappoint Me when she turns back. *Oh, girl, turn back.*

Don't believe the lie that you messed up too much to be fixed. Don't believe the distorted, twisted, hurtful daggers that tell you it is too late, too late, for you. Yes, there are things you did you wish you didn't. There are things I saw done to you that make my heart still ache and cry.

I only intend good for you, daughter. I only plan and speak goodness and hope. Even in the world's disappointments, I am bigger, and I bring a new way to look at the old. I replace all old with new. *There is nothing I don't see—nothing that breaks your heart that I don't care about.*

Say it aloud, girl, how you are tired. Say it aloud, girl, how you hope for more. I love giving more—more of Me, more love, more joy. I am in all places, and I redeem and bring beauty to all pasts. *Yours, daughters. I bring hope and joy to yours.*

You Have a Helper

But the Helper, the Holy Spirit, whom the Father will send in my name, he will teach you all things and bring to your remembrance all that I have said to you — John 14:26

MY DAUGHTER, there are things you know are true—things you can't see, things you can't touch. You read my words in pages held together, all stacked, one by one. You read the stories of my presence in my children's lives. You read about my promises. You see the words upon the page, listen to the sound of them expressed aloud. But what do they mean to you? Am I a God you see around you? Do you breathe Me in, this day?

You hear my name in sermons, read about Me in books. You hear my name tossed around on the lips of believers and unbelievers alike. A believer? A phrase so familiar . . . What is that? What does it mean to believe in something—in Me—as it requires so much faith?

I ask you to wait and trust Me. I tell you to not fear and look for where I am . . . Yes, even in the believing in something yet to be fully seen, you can still see Me. You can still feel Me. And I want to show you where.

There is a place, deep within you, that has eyes that see what is true. My Counselor, within you, the Holy Spirit, gives light, illuminating uncertainty, eradicating doubt, pushing forth understanding to what the world, on its own, can never understand.

This world is not meant to make sense, without the eyes and ears of my Counselor within you, guiding you to see and love and act in ways that do.

You see, it is up to you—my heart within you—to make sense in this misunderstood world. It is your task to see most clearly, from the place where my Counselor resides with you. It is your task to live, to act, from that place, from the understanding I give you about loving whom I say.

You have a Guide who knows Me and shows you the way to live. And it will not align with the ways of this world.

Listen deeply now. Pull in close to hear my whispers: Practice recognizing my voice so when you hear it, you can act. And do it with confidence, hearing Me and seeing me, even yet.

Someday there will be so much more to see, to hear, to understand. But you have enough now. I give you enough to know how to live and love now. Trust Me. Live that life now. Carry Me into the world.

For You, I Have So Much More

I will be found by you . . . and I will restore your fortunes and gather you from all the nations and all the places where I have driven you — Jeremiah 29:14

I KNOW THE WORD *story* carries with it so many emotions, so much heaviness, but relief, too. I know in your head you want words and memories to make sense. You want things to line up, and it is tough to not have answers, to not be able to explain the reason behind this happening, the cause of this event.

What if you knew more than you did? What if you could give an answer to the whys of your heart? What if you didn't have to struggle with weakness, with inadequacy, on your own? Can you imagine where that would lead you? *Do you trust how I protect your heart?*

I protect you, and I push you on, too. I lead you, but it is your choice whether or not to follow. I give you vision, just enough, to see where I am and know where I go, with you. One foot in front of the other. Why do you need to know more? Do you? Do you need to know more to believe Me more? Do you need to see more to know I am here, whispering to you, loving you, guiding you? *My daughter, you are not alone.*

My daughter, you have what it takes, my creation, my dear one, to follow Me.

My daughter, you are the only one of you I've made. There is just one. Only one, my dear. You are my crafted jewel, my sparkling flower, my glistening water as it falls from heaven. *You delight Me, child.*

Please don't look away, believe this is too good to be true. You feel that way to Me, you know . . . too good to be true. You are radiant and captivating and you need only stand with Me, watching where I beckon you, knowing I am the sure place for your legs to stand.

So, rest now. And then rise up. When you believe, a little more, choosing these words, my love for you, as true, you are on your way to a deeper place I have for you. *I have so much more for you, child.*

I Want to Show You All I Have

The Lord upholds all who are falling and raises up all who are bowed down
— Psalm 145:14

DAUGHTER, I speak confidence in you. I speak love in you. I know how you feel when you mess up, when you think of yourself first, when you don't trust Me, when you run after what you think you need and not what I know is best for your heart.

Oh, girl, confess your heart to Me, pour out your heart to Me. Keep turning, keep looking. Keep turning over your heart for Me. I want to show you what is underneath the choices you make away from Me.

When you choose selfishness instead of Me, you forget who I am. When you choose greed instead of Me, you idolize this world. When you choose envy instead of Me, you doubt I have given you enough and believe I am a God who doesn't care for His children.

When you choose judgment instead of forgiveness, hard-heartedness instead of kindness, self-indulgence instead of self-forgetfulness, I am forgotten, too.

When you choose to keep ignoring Me, reading my words but following your own path, you are blind to my steps in front of you, deaf to my words whispered in you, closed off from possibility of new directions, new hope, new places where I want to take you.

Hear this: You are not stuck. You can be moved. You can change. More hope is right around the corner. More possibility and further direction.

I want to show you more of what I have for you. I want to have you trust Me more. I want to take you in deeper, deeper still. My love has no end, the possibilities of hope and future strength in Me is beyond what you can see now.

So you need to keep turning over those things that feel safe and hold you back from trusting Me more. You need to stay close and be willing to move into uncomfortable and unfamiliar places with Me.

Do you want to know what awaits you, child? Do you want to know what is around the bend?

Keep listening. Keep confessing. Keep reaching and looking and going deeper.

I am with you. I move you in deeper. I want to show you all I have.

Don't Waste This Life With Fear

When I am afraid, I put my trust in you. In God, whose word I praise, in God I trust; I shall not be afraid. What can flesh do to me?
— Psalm 56: 3-4

DAUGHTER, there is a battle raging for your heart—a heart already captured, a war already won. But still, the battle continues, the fighting and luring you away while I woo you. I only woo you to Me, your Father who knows you and watches you and adores you. I don't force you to believe Me. I don't protect you from all harms of this world; although it is true, still, with Me you are safe.

I don't always step in and save you from your thoughts, full of fear and doubt and wondering. But I know your thoughts, and I woo you to consider the truth and security of my ways.

What is safety worth? What is security and a life removed of doubt and fear? Can you imagine yourself living this way?

You can't will this, child. You can't decide you want this safe life and have it granted to you. I ask you to keep your eyes on Me. I ask you to keep your ears tuned to my truth. I ask you to walk next to Me, measuring steps so when I ask you to go—do that unfamiliar and uncomfortable thing you've never done before—you don't hesitate because you have become so used to walking with Me.

Walk with Me to learn to trust Me more. Let Me show you what I see when I look at you. Let Me calm you, as you keep your eyes on Me. Let Me be your familiar place, your source of energy and inspiration and passion and joy.

Let Me reveal in you more of Me, more of the true, unharnessed beautiful, wild you who is unafraid of what comes next because *I will be what's next. I am what's next, child.*

Don't worry about details regarding how to live your life safely. Simply choose to be trained by

Me. I am your coach, your teacher, your rest, your energy, your drive, your passion, your fire, your water and food and air. *I am it.*

Lay yourself down again. I am here. With you. You waste this life with fear.

You are Beautiful

I praise you, for I am fearfully and
wonderfully made. Wonderful are your works;
my soul knows it very well — Psalm 139:14

MY DAUGHTER, you are the one I made. You are
the one I crafted. You are the one I adorn with
garlands, with beauty I see, with beauty that sweeps
Me off my feet. I love you. *I love you.*

And there is not guilt and cost and
expectation in it. I love you because I do. You can't
alter it. You can't change Me. You are what I have
made, and I love what I have made.

Look up now, not down. I mean this: I love you. Like this. How you are. *Right now.*

There is nothing to chase down, my love. There is nothing to earn or improve or repair. I create. I heal what I have made. Let me lean in, place my hand upon your heart.

I was there when you believed, for the first time, you weren't beautiful. I was there, the second time, and the next time, too. I want you to know, I was there.

I was there when my daughter, whom I crafted, whom I adore, whom I formed and designed and shape ever still, believed she was less than what she should be. Less perfect, less valued, less worthy than . . . Less than whom? Less than what, my daughter?

You are beautiful because I made you. You are exquisite because I shaped you. You are worthy because I say so. I chose you. I chose to make you. *You.* And daughter, I don't make mistakes.

My love, hold my hand. See how I extend it to you, and I love to be with you. My beautiful one. My daughter.

What Love Is

Father, if you are willing, remove this cup
from me. Nevertheless, not my will, but yours,
be done— Luke 22:42

MY LOVELY ONE. Do you know how I love to call
you that? You ask Me about my Son and his sacrifice
and my sacrifice. And I help you picture it. I help
you imagine.

Yes, I hid my face that day. Yes, I let the sky
tremble, the earth shake. All of heaven wanted to
explode. A battle waged, a victory won, a sacrifice:
what love is. One of the pictures of love.

Yes, love is sacrifice. Yes, love is putting self on the altar, giving yourself back to Me.

Love is giving yourself to Me. The eyes of the created looking to the Creator, the beginning of death and the beginning of life. You are born through Me. I give you life. No one else. You can find life nowhere else.

Are you willing to let yourself die to be born again, with Me? What needs to be sacrificed? Of what are you willing to let go? What do you hold tightly? What seems impossible—creates in you fear—to give to Me, to entrust to Me, to let Me take it and give you peace?

My Son's death and life and sacrifice and resurrection is enough. Just once. *The birthing of love once more.*

Come and give Me all of you. Let love live in you. Hold nothing back. *I am coming now.* My eyes on you.

Oh, lovely one, I know you want all I have to give.

Your New Habit

These things God has revealed to us through
the Spirit. For the Spirit searches everything,
even the depths of God. For who knows a
person's thoughts except the spirit of that
person, which is in him? So also no one
comprehends the thoughts of God except the
Spirit of God — 1 Corinthians 2: 10-11

MY DEAR ONE, here we are, beginning again. I
know you can feel lost, broken, distracted, weary,
and downcast. I know you can feel overwhelmed and
lonely and confused about the next step. There

always feels like a next step, right? There always feels like there is another thing to do, another obligation to fulfill, another task to complete.

I know you hear words about trusting Me and resting with Me and surrendering to Me and looking to Me. I tell you these things, I know.

I know you wonder how to do that and even if you are capable. Habits are familiar. Routines feel safe. Starting from scratch? Abandoning all you know and believed before about how to do things well, successfully? That feels radical, uncomfortable, risky. *I* feel risky.

Losing your life to gain Me feels the riskiest of all. I know. *I know you.*

I know when you sit and when you rise. I know your every thought, your every worry—every pause and breath and turn of your heart.

If the one who knows you better than anyone says He is safe, what else can be trusted?

Let Me rewrite the schedule, the agenda for this day. Let Me paint you a picture of open-space freedom where trusting Me becomes the new habit—the new heart born again in the woman I created. You are only as strong as you are weak. You are only as fearless and free as you are willing . . . willing to not have the answers, the plan . . . and surrender.

Yes, I have more to tell you. I have more to show you. Keep listening. I'll quiet your heart.

You Stand Because I Stand

Have I not commanded you? Be strong and courageous. Do not be frightened, and do not be dismayed, for the Lord your God is with you wherever you go — Joshua 1:9

YOU ARE MY DEAR ONE. Every act of love, every term of affection, every caress, every high-five, every smile is because of Me. I create everything good. I create love. I bring forth love.

You are not like trees pushed over, roots pulled up from the ground. They lay there, roots exposed, vulnerable, thirsty and desperate, drying up for lack of care, lack of nourishment, attention, love. *I bring forth love in you, dear one.*

I bring forth goodness, and I raise you up to stand, to not cower and hide, but to stand. You can lean against Me when you stand. You can feel like crying and hiding and running and turning far, far away, while I stand.

You stand because I stand with you. You are a warrior, a gentle, fierce, mighty, heroic, beautiful, glorious warrior in my name. I foster in you beauty and gentleness and humbleness, a full heart with me. And this is all, only because . . . with you, I stand.

I stand amidst storms and droughts. I stand through heartache and sickness and loss and death. I stand when you cannot. I stand because you cannot. I stand because I want to. *I like being here with you.*

I come, rescued one. I come, beautiful one. I come, delightful one. I come, fierce one. You stand because in you I've placed roots nourished by my love. Held, steadfast by my love.

My love is what is strong. My love is what holds you secure. Keep thinking on Me, eyes on Me. I can help you lean on Me. I can help you love Me. I am the creator of love. *There is more than enough love to go around.*

So, ask Me. Ask Me for more love in your heart. Ask Me to help you lean into Me. Ask Me to

loop

help you see what I see—what your roots look like,
how I care for you, how I do more than just help you
to stand.

Want to Wrestle?

O God, save me by your name, and vindicate me by your might — Psalm 54:1

LET'S KEEP THIS SIMPLE. There is a pace, a rhythm to how I work in you. I know you want to rush it, to feel fully free. I place that longing within you to search for Me, a longing that cannot be replaced but can be filled with other things, other commitments.

Oh, daughter, what does it look like to be committed to Me? Let Me tell you.

There is waiting. A lot of waiting. At least that is what it feels like.

It feels like I am stalling, that I am busy doing other things and can't attend to you or I am pushing you to wrestle with Me into discomfort.

Wrestling, by its nature, is uncomfortable. But let me tell you more about wrestling. It is full body contact. It is arms wrapped around. It is holding on tight and tumbling and maintaining a firm grasp on your opponent.

I am willing to wrestle with you. I am willing to stay here, in the arena, with you. I am willing to be with you, reassuring you I am here.

The waiting isn't stagnation when you are wrestling with Me. I would rather you wrestle with Me, want to push back against Me, in frustration or anger or fear, than turn your back and not engage all together.

Daughter, I want to engage. I love for you to tell Me what you think, how you are mad or hurt or frustrated or scared. I want to hear you cry out, see you reach for Me, look around, seeking to find Me so you can grab hold of Me—right here—and head into the arena where we can have it out.

I want to have all of you. You are not too much. You are not too much for Me to handle. And I am strong enough to hold you while you cling to Me, not sure if you want to hang on or let go.

want to wrestle?

Keep hanging on, girl. No matter what, I am holding you the whole time.

Let Me Tell You a Story

God is faithful, by whom you were called into the fellowship of his Son, Jesus Christ our Lord — 1 Corinthians 1:9

MY DAUGHTER, where do I begin? Let me tell you a story. There once was a little girl, with eyes sparkling bright and lips that stretched toward pink cheeks when she smiled. She liked to reach her hands up high, fingers outstretched, and the wind would brush back her hair. She knew she was delighted in, that she was magnetic, that when I looked at her, I was captivated.

She liked to run through forest where she had never been before. She felt safe. There was no place she couldn't go where I wouldn't be. So, she ran and jumped and laughed, and the music of her laughter made my heart swell. It was the music of her heart full and pure and beautiful.

She was rescued, and she didn't know it. So, she felt free. Her feet were bare, her toes touching the soft textures of meadow grass and the smooth rocks collected at the side of streams. She was seen and known and loved. She ran freely, collecting different sizes of rocks and flowers, along the way.

She ran unencumbered, unhesitatingly, knowing where she was going but never knowing the way. I was with her, the two of us, keeping pace along the path. I would protect her off the path, and she fell sometimes. But she knew she was not alone, and she was not afraid.

This little girl grew, in strength and with words. She knew joy and contentment. She knew where to rest her head, and she knew that when a battle called her to stand and fight she could do it. For she knew I went with her.

This little girl heart is what is most beautiful about you. It is what lives within you. It is where I invite you to come in deeper, look for Me more, let Me come and rescue you again. And again. For you know now you have been rescued. You remember, I am the one who makes you free.

Oh, my darling girl, my rescued one, my girl in white who captivates Me and grows strong and ever more confident in how I love you. Raise your head now, dear one. The road has been long and hard, but still, you are my mighty, beautiful girl who holds my hand and likes to walk barefoot, in streams.

You're the One I Choose to Love

He chose us in him before the foundation of the world, that we should be holy and blameless before him — Ephesians 1:4

MY DAUGHTER, I am your strength. No matter where you go and where you turn, my love for you does not change. *I want* to be with you.

I am not obligated to love you because I am your Father. It is not something I have to do. But I do.

I do not change. And so my love does not change. *I want* to love you. I am what I am, and I love what I do.

I choose to be with you, and *I choose* to love you. *I choose* to be your strength. I do what I do because I am who I am. You can count on Me.

You can count on Me to love you no matter where you go or what you do. And the belief I give you in Me, your heart to choose Me or turn away from Me, will help you believe. I can deepen your belief in my love, and I can help your unbelief.

So do not despair. Do not worry that your thoughts about Me bring Me close and push Me away. My love is what draws Me to you. And my love draws you to Me.

Some things you cannot control. And isn't that better?

So, what do you want to tell Me now? What do you want to ask Me? I love being with you. I love how we spend time together.

We're Pretty Good
Together

*For you are all children of light, children of
the day. We are not of the night or of the
darkness — I Thessalonians 5:5*

MY DAUGHTER, you need Me like the flowers
need sun, like the earth quakes and needs to be
quieted, like the sand cries out for a drop of rain.
You need Me to write truth again, in the places
where it has been forgotten. You need Me to awaken
faith and stir the lukewarm so it heats or freezes so

that my children who don't know Me don't confuse Me with another nice person on the street.

I am not nice, with a smile on my face each day. But I am joy-filled. I am not mellow or calm all the time. But I am peace. I am secure in who I am. I am the rock, the lion who roars, the light that shines, the beginning and the only way darkness can end.

I am the end. The end of suffering. The end of angst. The end of fear. The end of death. The end of pain. The end of striving. The end of destruction for the sake of getting ahead. The end of comparison. The end of trying to fit in. The end of loneliness. The end of despair. The end of sickness. The end of confusion. The end of self-centeredness. The end of self.

You need Me in order to become yourself. You need Me because you are made for freedom. You need Me because you are holy, in my name, and I have designed you with a purpose, a purpose to help and to heal and to encourage and to love. You need Me to receive the joy that is yours, that you were born to receive, for which you were designed to love. You need Me because you are thirsty and hungry and craving more Life, more hope, more freedom, more joy. You are made to desire Me and do the things you have been made to do.

I want to tell you what those things are and who you are. My daughter. My delight.

You're the Only One

And the Lord will guide you continually and satisfy your desire in scorched places and make your bones strong; and you shall be like a watered garden, like a spring of water, whose waters do not fail — Isaiah 58:11

MY DARLING, you don't have to worry about how to distinguish yourself, with Me. You don't have to worry about standing out, being noticed. You don't have to try so hard. I see you. You can't make Me love you more.

It is true that things hold you back from receiving my love for you. You hold on so tightly, too tightly to fear. You think too much about figuring out what you don't know. You stop seeing what is right in front of you, what I've given you to do, to live out, to experience during this moment.

This day, this gift right here. Open up the gift, my daughter. The gift of this moment with Me.

I love to guide you, to show you bits of what is ahead. I tell you what you need to know. I whisper who you are into your heart, and you rise up, delighted in and true—truly you—when you let go of trying to be like her . . . or like her, over there. Be fully *you*, who I've created you to be.

I put people around you to guide you, shepherd you towards Me. And I ask you to shepherd children to Me, too. I don't leave you alone, for I have good plans for you. Plans for you unlike any other.

You are unlike anyone else, my daughter. See what's around you. Know I see you. Live like you know who you are.

I Let You Choose

And I will be a father to you, and you shall be sons and daughters to me — Corinthians 6:18

MY DAUGHTER, I see you. I know where you've been. I know where you're going. I know you are grown, and that you are afraid and you still feel a little girl inside. Do you know I call you to be free? Do you know it breaks my heart to see you in such pain? Do you know there is nowhere you can run where I can't find you? Do you know that if you run, I will run with you, next to you? Do you know I love to never leave your side?

I know it hurts, my love. I know there are
places you wish you could just wish away. I know you
are weary, and you are tired of trying so hard to be
loved. I know you feel you don't deserve it, my love,
even though I tell you again and again.

I know how words just don't matter much—
that words are only received by a heart open and soft
and ready. I make you ready, child. I soften you and
move you and do not neglect you. My heart burns
for you; and my Son, with his blood pouring out,
sacrificed his life so you could be free.

And you are free, my love. It is a lie that you
are not free.

You can choose to remain enslaved, by sin.
You can choose to remain tied up, by lies that tell
you you are small and worth nothing. You can
choose to live tired and forgotten and striving.

This is not my plan for you. This is not
living, child. This is dying. This is death. Living
enslaved by lies and caring more about what anyone
else thinks—anyone at all—more than what I think,
more than what I tell you, is sin. It is believing a lie
that enslaves you and keeps you separate from Me.

Daughter, do you feel separate from Me? Do
I feel close? I am. I am close. I am here. I am with
you. I am for you.

I am the Father who runs towards you, with
open arms. I am the Father who holds his daughter
and swings her around and lifts her high and gives

158

her legs on which to stand. I am the Father who gives you a life where you rise. You stand tall. You stand tall when you know I love you and you are chosen and you don't take your eyes off Me.

Keep your eyes on Me, child. Just Me. I can silence the lies, if you'll let Me. I can quiet your heart, if you want Me to. I can kiss your cheeks and show you how the sun shines on you. But I let you choose.

I let you choose.

Can You Stay?

My presence will go with you, and I will give you rest — Exodus 33:14

I WILL SIT HERE WITH YOU, you know. You don't have to feel guilty about doing anything. You don't have to get up now. You don't have to figure out how to make this day special, how to make it worth something.

You don't have to have a plan or an answer. You don't have to feel confident or put together or beautiful. I know who you are. I know what you're worth.

160

can you stay?

I know where you're going and where you've been and what it takes for you to breathe. Yes, breathe. I know your inner working, the intricacies of your makeup. And you don't need to prove anything to Me. I've got you. And that is enough.

There are days when I've given you something to do, an invitation to go forward, to go deeper in. And you will know when I ask you whether or not you'd like to join Me there. *But what about here? What about right now, here, with Me, child?* My daughter, do you see this moment? Do you see how I hold it? Do you see how you take my breath away?

I am with you, and I ask you to stay. I am for you, and I ask you to listen. I am before you, and I ask you to see. I care for you. It is okay to rest. I made you. Nothing you do can make Me regret it.

So stay with Me, and I will equip you for more. Stay with Me, and I will pour into you vision and wisdom and the steps, one by one, as you watch where my feet fall. You cannot go anywhere until you know where I am with you and how, with Me, it is always best for you to stay. For then we can go . . . and you won't have to have a bit of it figured out, my daughter.

I'm With You On This Road

Trust in the Lord with all your heart, and do not lean on your own understanding. In all your ways acknowledge him, and he will make straight your paths — Proverbs 3:5-6

MY DAUGHTER, you are no mistake. I made you with intention, I made you with your face in my mind, your voice in my ears. I made you with a name and with grace and with gifts only yours—your gifts my very gift to you.

You are not made with a pressure to perform, with an expectation to achieve. You are not made with a heaviness to bear around your neck, a weight to carry, a weariness of long days one after another.

I know the way with Me can feel hard. I know this road feels long. I am with you on the road, my dear. *I am with you on this road.*

Take steps now, where you can no longer see. Reach your hand out now, for I long to grab yours and hold tight. Lift those shoulders now; let me take that burden you carry.

Can you see me taking it? Can you see my hands upon your shoulders, the weight being lifted off? Can you feel shackles being cut? Can you feel the things you can't, with your eyes, see?

I am for you, my child. And I do not ask you to go places where I will not be. *Only go where I am.* Even though you can't see the next steps, I do. And I go ahead, and I know when the path is clear.

Just follow Me, my daughter. I know this road, this one marked out for you. You have choices about where to go, whether to turn right or to turn left. But ask Me where I am. And trust I give you recognition for the One who made you, for the One who designed your heart, for the One who knows His daughter and the details of the road, for her, ahead.

Are You Coming?

God, the Lord, is my strength; he makes my feet like the deer's; he makes me tread on my high places — Habakkuk 3:19

I USHER YOU INTO MY PRESENCE. I come, to overwhelm you, all your senses, all your memories. I am bigger than your greatest fear. I am bigger than your greatest hope.

It's time to not be timid now. It's time to let Me come rushing in, my presence energizing you, bringing you forward, leading you to what I have.

are you coming?

I have healing for your heart. I have healing
for your past. I have hope for your tomorrow. I have
hope for your today.

You can stay in the same place, if you want
to. You don't have to trust Me. You don't have to let
Me in. You can hear my voice here and still hesitate,
unsure what loving Me, what trusting me, will
require. You can let fear and uncertainty be your
guide, and not my voice, my greatest desire for your
good, my richest love for you.

Do you anticipate Me coming? Do you look
for Me and expect for Me to show up? Do you await
Me, eyes open, heart ready? Are you willing and
ready to follow Me, when I say to you, "Daughter,
rise, I have more for you; it is time for you to lift
your head. It is time for you to go forward and let
yourself be rescued and then go and rescue, too?"

I created you with strength within you. I
created you with beauty tangible. I created you with
goodness and love pouring into you to pour out.

You are no small thing, while a wisp of
breath. You inhabit my glory. You inhabit Me, and I
inhabit you. This—the place we inhabit together—is
the place where you can move around, feel freedom,
breathe in joy and let my light, for others, shine.

I made you to be humble, but not meek. I
created you to walk with lifted head, proclaiming my
name, showing this world you are loved. For the
reality of being loved and known and made and
wanted and perfected in faith is what allows you to

go forward, grasping hold of my hand, pulling other daughters out of darkness, too.

Are you coming?

I Know It Hurts

Instead of your shame there shall be a double portion; instead of dishonor they shall rejoice in their lot; therefore in their land they shall possess a double portion; they shall have everlasting joy — Isaiah 61:7

MY DAUGHTER, I see you. You are always new to Me. You are always interesting to Me. I never tire of you. I never wonder what's next. I like staying here. I like being with you.

Your life is not small. You are not small. You inhabit me. You inhabit where I live, where my heart resides. This is your truest home. This is where you breathe. This is where you drink. This is where you are sustained.

When you are in the place where you are sustained, there is no next thing. When you know you are home, and you belong, there is no other home. When you know you are loved, and you know whom you call family, and you know your name is Daughter, Beloved, Chosen One, you can rest, and you can live, and you can be free.

My daughter, maybe there isn't the next thing. Maybe there isn't a better place than where I am. You are the daughter I named, the daughter I designed, with purpose, with beauty planned. You are the daughter with promise. You are the daughter I love.

Cry out now. Say aloud the desires of your heart. Tell Me what makes you sad, how you are hurt, how you are angry and wish your life were different, how you wish you were different, how you fear you disappoint Me, how you wish you didn't make that mistake . . .

I hear you . . . But you know what? These things are not what I see. These memories—of fear and pain—are moments shaping you, opportunities to see Me. Things happen I never planned. I planned you, but there are circumstances that happen to you I never planned. And I am sorry. And I suffer with you, when you, my daughter, are in pain.

I know it hurts

Know you are seen. Know you are loved.
Know you are where I want to be, no matter what.

Is This Where You Want to Be?

As for that in the good soil, they are those who, hearing the word, hold it fast in an honest and good heart, and bear fruit with patience — Luke 8:15

THERE IS THE UNCOVERING NOW. I uncover you, lifting you up from the place where you are. Placing your feet on new soil. When you are placed in this new place, look for Me. I know you cry rescue. I know you cry peace. You crave slowing. You crave my hand upon your heart.

When you are replanted, notice the soil. Ask Me what it needs. I have designed you. And because I have designed you, you crave Me. Because I have designed you and planted you and watered you and adored you, your new place will have Me there. I will fill it up, if you want Me to.

Would you ask Me to? Would you ask Me to fill up the space where you are?

I have come for you, and I remind you how deep my love is, the height and depth of my love. I am the strength you crave, the energy you desire. I am healing. I am newness. Come, be planted and look around. Look at Me, where I am. And then . . . and then, I will show you what I see.

For where you are planted is where I want you to see. I want you to see with my eyes, my heart. I put you here to not stay a stump, a dry stalk stuck in cracked ground. I ask you if you want to be watered and fed and nourished with rich soil. Do you?

I ask if you want to be fed with holy water, my life pouring in so it overflows. Drink of the stream, my daughter. Look where you are planted. See the richness I bring. You can't see it unless you ask Me to give you my eyes, my heart. You won't see the fertile ground. Let Me show you.

loop

See my hand? May we go?

Keep Fighting

In all circumstances take up the shield of
faith, with which you can extinguish all the
flaming darts of the evil one; and take the
helmet of salvation, and the sword of the
Spirit, which is the word of God
— Ephesians 6:16-17

MY DAUGHTER, I am here. I have given you a
heart that knows what is good, what it needs to live
and thrive. You struggle against this true part of you,
and that is where I come. I lay my hand on you and
tell you I am enough . . . and I can take it from here.

173

Don't be afraid of the struggle of self, the part of you that wants to rise up and fight surrender. I will help you fight. For remember, I have already fought the battle and won. What I make is good and beautiful—and rebellion against Me can be conquered.

Let the part of you that yearns for Me be what you heed—to make decisions, to make choices in how you spend your day, your time. Don't be discouraged by mistakes you make, and the way you fall.

Keep fighting, for I have already fought against darkness for the sake of your life. Keep fighting, for I have chosen you and you are worth dying for.

Keep fighting, because I have come for you, and I do not leave you, even when the fighting feels too hard and you feel overwhelmed. Keep fighting, for there is more light to come, more hope to come, more joy to come, for you.

I am sorry for the hardship of this battle, my love. The outcome, at the end, is good. Because I fight. Because I fought.

I stand with you, seeing the beauty of what I have prepared for you, beyond this battlefield. Keep pushing on.

Keep fighting.

The Way You Dance

Therefore, as you received Christ Jesus the Lord, so walk in him — Colossians 2:6

DAUGHTER, I LOVE YOUR GIFTS. I love what you are equipped to do. I love how you are made and the way you see. You are needed for the way you see.

The way you love is unique to everyone else. You are needed to reach out, for I give you eyes to see things no one else will notice. Your heart beats fast, its own rhythm. And I love how it is made to beat in alignment with Me.

The way you move with Me is a pace that feels like dance. You move with beauty and with grace and with light that cannot be contained. It is made to be seen. You are made to be seen by Me, and I see you, and I delight in you, and I love how you do it.

My eyes are on you, and your eyes are made to be on what you love. And I can show you how to love Me more. What you are made to love, with Me, will be blessed by the fullness of my love. All this will be done through the unique way you see, with the unique way your eyes are on Me.

You love what you are made to love when you keep your eyes on Me. For then you see what you are made to see, your dance steps in sync with Me. You turn and dip and bend and twirl, and we keep step together. There is music, now, when we dance, to bless the ones you see.

Let's, together, invite them in. For I let you see possibility. I let you see hope. I let you see light.

Who needs to be invited in? Whom have I made you to see? Who wants to join in—learning the steps to their unique dance, with Me?

Time for You to Rise

Because he holds fast to me in love, I will
deliver him; I will protect him, because he
knows my name — Psalm 91:14

MY DAUGHTER, don't be afraid. I am here. I
know how hard it is to feel, sometimes. This
moment, I know, is difficult to let yourself feel.
Don't hold back. Don't protect yourself from feeling,
your emotions this way and that. This is a gift from
Me, the way your heart swings from high to low. I
am the constant one. I keep you still.

There are things you will have to face now. I
know you want to bury your head, and I let you do

that, your head buried on my chest. But know when you lift your head, I will be there to help you to rise. And you will rise, and your feet will find firm footing, and you will square your shoulders and take one step forward, and then another, and you will find you know your way.

There is much ahead, and the path does not always seem clear. But I help you to rise. I go ahead, and I help you to rise. And when you stumble, I will help you to stand again. And when you are scared, I will firm your trembling lip and I will navigate you through the storm of emotions and I will quiet your quivering heart.

You are fierce and gentle. You are beautiful and strong. You are chosen and delighted in. You are all I've made you to be. I took everything from you that has kept you from rising. I have taken everything that makes you feel small and unsure and hesitant.

You can go forward, to the places I lead you. And you will know who you are. My daughter, the one who knows her Father, the one who knows her name.

Fully You

Whom have I in heaven but you? And there is
nothing on earth that I desire besides you
— Psalm 73:25

MY DAUGHTER. Those two words are not small.
My . . . mine . . . what belongs to Me, what I call my
own. Daughter, family, a closer tie than any flesh,
any blood. I begin here, reminding you who you are.

When you hear Me, from the true place that
responds to my voice and knows who you are, you
begin to think about yourself less. You strive less.
You have nothing to prove. I start here, my whisper,

my daughter, to ask you to let go of insecurity, let go
of stories that are false, let go of memories that can't
be changed. Begin your day thinking about who you
are, as that is how you remember your connection to
Me.

Nothing separates us, my dear, nothing
except what you want to keep separate. We are
united because I have made it so.

I see all you've done, and I cleanse you. You
are white as snow. I recently whispered to you it was
time to rise. I have come for you. You are chosen.
You are my daughter. I have made you, beautiful
one, to claim your place. I ask you to abandon
waiting for more than what I offer you, abandon
searching for more than what I give.

Trust Me. Look to Me. Now listen.

I place within you longing. Pursue this
longing. Don't ignore this. But pay attention for
what it is you long. Ask yourself if you long for more,
from a conviction of knowing who you are. Notice if
you long to be more whom I've created you to be,
and not someone different. Notice if you long to go
further, with Me, using the talents and passions I've
placed within you—or if you are trying to prove
yourself, if you wish you were more loved, more
liked, more noticed, more cared for, more desired,
more perfect.

There are gifts within you, child, gifts I long
for you to see. I say it again, daughter, *rise*. Raise your

head and remember who you are and know your place and how I've chosen you and how the beginning of freedom and self-forgetfulness and love for Me is knowing who you are.

Mine. My *daughter*. My beloved. Most cherished. Most loved. Most fully you.

You are Not in the Dark

The night is far gone; the day is at hand. So then let us cast off the works of darkness and put on the armor of light — Romans 13:12

THIS IS NOT THE END, you know. Even though, this day, it may feel like it. This is the day I begin again. The day I begin again in you.

     Your weariness is only temporary. Your sadness is fleeting, even though it feels like it will never end, never subside, never go away. You, my love, are sunshine. You are kisses of light upon flower petals when they stretch for light, for Me. *I'm here.*

I am present, my daughter. I kiss your face with my hope. I grasp hold of sorrow with a single hand and I usher it away, bit by bit. I know you want it washed away with a quick brush, a dashing movement. I could do that.

But I want you to look to Me, now, child. I want you to wait on Me and recognize Me when I come for you. I want you to *practice recognizing beauty and hope.* I want you to wait on moments where hope feels too far away to imagine it as real. And then I want you to throw out doubt, just throw it out to the depths of hell, where sin was cast with the last breath of my Son's words, choosing Me, seeking Me, looking to Me.

I cannot stop loving you. *I cannot stop.* I cannot stop chasing you, pursuing you, looking for you. Oh, girl, you are not my lost one. You are not hopeless or far from Me. I am here, and I come to hold you and lift your head to the light shining brightly on your face. Do you see it? Do you see how light comes to shine? Do you see how it came for you and how it rescued you and how light shines through all darkness so darkness, with Me close, is no more?

Do you know how all shadows are chased away with a choice to see Me? *You can do this.* You can see Me. You can see Me moving you, one step at a time, from this place where you feel you need rescue and I show you how I have already come and I come again. I never stop coming for you, my daughter. You are not alone, and it is not too late, and you have not done anything to chase Me away. You cannot chase Me away.

You are beloved and holy because I have made you so. You are lovely and clean because I have made you that way. You are brand new and adored and shame cannot find you. Find your name written on my hand; respond to my voice; know the name called out to you, in the light—my voice calling out when darkness feels all around but I show you I am here. In the light. Darkness isn't around Me. And you are with Me. So darkness is not there, too.

Light all around my love. Light all around.

Your Friend

Behold, I stand at the door and knock. If anyone hears my voice and opens the door, I will come in to him and eat with him, and he with me — Revelation 3:20

I KNOW it feels hard to hear Me sometimes. I know you wonder how you can become more adept at listening, keen to my voice within you. My whispers are always loud enough for you to hear, but quiet enough so that they can be ignored, too.

Have you considered how this might be the best kind of relationship—a relationship where the friend doesn't barge in, demanding to be noticed, shouting to be heard? That can be a lot of noise. And communication, then, is only clamor—not solicitude, not kindness, not fortification for your heart.

I am the friend who asks to be invited in. I am the friend in the quiet, the quiet within you, the guest outside the door knocking, waiting. I am here, not far away. And I don't tell you I am waiting to be invited in because I want you to feel guilty or sad or discouraged. I am not telling you I stand, outside, waiting, for the purpose of making you feel you need to work harder, listen better, be a kinder daughter to Me.

I am your friend, and I love you. And I desire friends who love, who nurture, who pour kindness into one another. You can hear Me. You can be that friend, with Me..

I want you to know I am the friend who will not disappoint. I am the friend who will be strong when you need Me to be. I am the friend who will give you words of hope when you feel sad or disappointed. I am the friend who knows what you mean when you say "I am dying inside" or "I am so alone" and you are lost and afraid of the quiet.

I am the friend who can be heard, even amidst noise. Your heart can be tuned to Me, in any situation. But in the quiet, it can be easiest to hear Me. You can be busy and bustling around. But remember I am the friend who equips you to love others. And without you letting Me in, into your relationships, into your work, into your moments of doing and going and trying, you will feel hollow inside. You will feel alone.

I am the friend who knows everything about you and knows you can, indeed, hear Me.

Listen. Shall I come in?

You are Beginning to See

> Though you have not seen him, you love him.
> Though you do not now see him, you believe
> in him and rejoice with joy that is
> inexpressible and filled with glory
> — 1 Peter 1:8

MAY WE START HERE, my love? May we start with your greatest desire? May we start our time here, together, thinking a bit about how I've made you, and whether or not you like what you see?

Desire, yearning, awakening to passion, awakening to beginning . . . each occurs when you can let yourself see glimpses of the beauty of you I see. Oh, my daughter, *I see you. I like what I see.* When I thought of you, I knew who you'd be, this day. I knew the story, and the unfolding, and the journey, and how it has been hard.

I am sorry it has been hard, but trust I don't leave you here, in a place of desolation, in a place where it is only desert. I don't leave you here to wander forever. I come and rescue and lead you with my right hand holding you fast. I do not forsake you or refuse healing or turn away when a hand is outstretched. I turn when a full heart, desperate for me, seeks healing, cries out for restoration.

Speak out truth now. *Speak it out, even if you don't yet believe it. I will help you believe.* I will help you believe I will rescue you. I will help you believe I am here. I will help you believe, with your whole heart, I am enough.

Where do you place your hope, my love? Where do you run when you are worn out and frazzled? To what do you turn for energy? How do you attempt to find the next plan? *Bend low now. See what I see.* Quiet your heart and let Me show you what I see. Let Me speak truth into your heart that you may know who you are and know you are not alone and know how I lead you to new, fragrant places. *See.*

loop

The land ahead is lush and you are cared for. You know how you are carried and valued and delighted in and seen.

You are the beautiful land, plentiful and rich and bountiful. Your heart is full and your life is full and your future is full and you are beginning now . . . You are beginning to *see*.

You Have Something to Say

Then those who feared the Lord spoke with one another. The Lord paid attention and heard them, and a book of remembrance was written before him of those who feared the Lord and esteemed his name — Malachi 3:16

FAIR ONE, I come for you. I come for you again. I do not tire of being close to you. I do not tire of leaning in, listening to your words, your cries, your pleas, your songs. I strengthen you. I equip you. I

restore you. I surround you with hope. I bring
people around you to show you hope. You have
brothers and sisters I want to show you, people
whose names I know and whom I delight in bringing
forth to you, whom I delight in you getting to know.

So open your eyes now. Be open and trust
Me. I protect your heart, when I am in the center of
community, with you. Do not fear trusting your
heart with another when I am in the center. I am the
safe place so you can take risks with your heart. Do
not fear. I am the safe place so you can be bold and
vulnerable and fearless.

You have a story all your own, with ups and
downs and things you regret, things you've done you
wish you could change. Ask Me into those places.
Let Me show you a new way to view these old stories.
There is a fresh story I want to give you, a fresh
perspective on every past thing you've done that you
regret.

There is hope everywhere, child. There is
hope in everything, in every moment, in every past,
in every future. The hope for the future exists in
Me—and I ask you to trust Me so I may show you
how I look at your past. When I show you your past,
I am asking you to trust Me in how I see you. And
how I see you is not at all how you see yourself.

I give you glimpses of beauty, glimpses of
glory, glimpses of hope and light. But the light that
shines all around you, the light that shines from

within you, the Spirit I give you to lead you and be your friend and carry you through these hard days, is what makes you beyond beautiful, my daughter. *You are beyond what you can imagine right now.*

There is light within you that cannot be contained, and that is the light that rewrites all past mistakes, rewrites all regrets, and gives you courage to go forward into the new story I give for you to share. Share with these people I bring, these people with whom you can trust you heart. Look for Me, ask Me where I am. Ask Me if I am with them. And if I am, go forward, daughter, and share that story of yours that will be a blessing to all who hear it. Because it is the story of hope, the story of light, the story of the two of us, so beautiful, together.

I've Written You a
Love Song

The Lord your God is in your midst, a mighty
one who will save; he will rejoice over you
with gladness; he will quiet you by his love; he
will exult over you with loud singing
— Zephaniah 3:17

I LOVE TO SIT HERE with you. We can sit, side by
side—you by my side. It is lovely here. Close your
eyes. Let me show you what I see . . . I usher you into
my company. I invite you to spend this day with me.

194

Right now, this moment. Stay here, where I am . . . Deep breath now, dear one. Oh, how you make me smile. You know you don't have to try so hard to be loved by me . . . I'm not going anywhere. Remember, I love to stay here, with you.

Maybe this will be enough for today? Maybe sitting here, with Me, will be enough? Sometimes the quiet place where we go can't be explained in words. Sometimes it is the place you know, deep within you, the picture I give you of where you most like to go, what you most like to do. It is the whisper most familiar, the love song so deep inside you you can easily not recognize it as the voice of Me singing. But I do. I love to sing over you, my dear.

Shall we stay here together, a little longer? Shall we wait together, your shoulder folded into my chest. Shall we rest? May I give you rest? It is time to slow now. It is time to stay close to Me. There is so much to do, I know. But is there? Do you trust your list of what needs to get done more than Me? It will not all get done. There will never be that perfect day to spend with Me. But this moment, this moment right here.

Come close, my daughter. I miss the slowing. I miss the gentle rhythm of moving, my step, then yours, my leaning, then yours. Let this be the season of slowing, of sitting with me. Come, with anticipation. Come, with expectation. Come, with excitement. Come, with time to spend with Me.

Come, with desire. Come, with surrender. Come, with longing. Come, with a seeking heart.

Come to Me, and I will sit down too. And we will sit together, side by side, and we will enjoy this day together. You will be so close you will hear the sound of my breathing. You will watch the movement of my lips when I speak. You will know the color of my eyes. And you will know the feel of my skin as I hold your hand in my own.

Can we sit together now, my dear?

Run Hard Now

Do you not know that in a race all the runners run, but only one receives the prize? So run that you may obtain it — 1 Corinthians 9:24

IT'S TIME TO AWAKE now, while I care for you, while I hold you and let you love. Awake, this day. Give thanks for what has been forgotten, for people I bring around you, for this unfolding day, for all the unknowns, for the possibilities. What do you hope is possible? What do you want to ask Me now?

There is no separation between us, now. The curtain has been torn and I am here, leaning in.

Your freedom and new day comes from living in my love. Know you are loved and respond to my love and my love pours out to everyone you see today.

When you let nothing separate us, when you hand over the sin that can't separate us unless you let it, you are free. And all the desires of loving others well, being present and sacrificing and surrendering and thinking of others more than yourself comes naturally.

Love is who you are when I am chosen and all separation with me is handed over. Hand yourself over, my daughter.

Jesus had the choice, to be handed over or not. He took all sin, but I didn't force him. It is impossible for him to not do my will when his life is one with me. You are capable of anything, and your life is full of possibility and joy and hope when you trust Me more than yourself, when you allow my strength to be your strength, when your weaknesses are no longer weaknesses but strengths, too.

I call you to awake and to go deeper still, in your trust of Me. I call you to live in the safe place of my love so you can go out and love others well. There are so many who don't know this hope you have, and I ask you to awake and sing loud the life I give you. You are the blessing. You are the one I chose to love and bless and carry forth the hope within you so others may hope and respond to my love by being blessed by the love I give you.

Remember, nothing stands between us, love. Be firm in your pursuit of Me. To awake means to fight hard the battle I've given you to fight—and remember, you do it for the sake of the ones I know are lost. I have found you. You are found. So, now awake; get going. Run hard for the ones I show you to love.

I show you how to love. I show you what it means to live awake.

Because You Know
the Way Home

For the Lord gives wisdom; from his mouth
come knowledge and understanding; he
stores up sound wisdom for the upright; he is
a shield to those who walk in integrity,
guarding the paths of justice and watching
over the way of his saints. Then you will
understand righteousness and justice and
equity, every good path — Proverbs 2:6-9

MY DAUGHTER, you never have to search far for
Me. You are released from searching, from believing

you don't have what it takes to be with Me, hear Me, live with Me. You are chosen. I chose you before the world was formed. You are the rescued one, and I delight in being with you. I equip you to hear Me, to be near me, to walk beside Me.

As my daughter, you are my heir, heir to a kingdom where you know, without question, you are home. I am your home. I am the place where you lay your head and where everything makes sense. You don't need to attempt to make sense of this world swirling around you—but I want you to feel it. I want you to feel for it. I want you to notice how it hurts and where there is need and how you are made, just as you are, chosen to live in this world, knowing it needs to know the way home.

You know the way home. You know the sound of beauty ringing, of hope coming in battle for your heart. You know pain and surrender and wanting more than what you can see.

Look close now. See Me. See Me seeing you. See Me looking at this world. Recognize its pain and its ache to know there is more—the more you know. Go deeper with Me now. Let Me show you more of what I see, how I feel, how you are the one who can go forward, brave one, into the path I've set aside, just for you.

There is a path for you, you know, a place where your feet know where to step and your hands know how to love. You have ideas and a heart designed for loving this person, right here, and this one, right here. The people in your life right now? Look closely now. Listen carefully now. You know how to love them. You know what to do next. Heed the whispers of your heart, the whispers that come from the place you know, the only place you can trust, the place where you began and begin again, the voice of Home.

You are designed for this—this moment, this moment of rescue and hope. I have come for you. Stay home. It is the only way to go out and bring others Home.

How to Get Through a Day

I know, O Lord, that the way of man is not in himself, that it is not in man who walks to direct his steps — Jeremiah 10:23

WATCH WHERE THE LIGHT SHINES now. Watch Me. Follow Me. Lift your head and stay focused on what I have. It is difficult to stay focused, so easy to get distracted, so easy to forget you are the one I love. I can help.

My daughter, it is a fight to stay close to Me. It is a choice you make each moment. Pay attention

to the rhythm of your days, the way you wake—what
you do when you first get up, what your first
thoughts are, how you approach what is for you to
do. Right when you wake, try turning over the plan
for your day to Me, first. Before you attempt to
accomplish one thing, ask Me what I think of your
plan. Can you imagine wiping your list clean, the
details scrawled out, and then rewriting it, in my
hand, my fingerprints upon the page? Are you
willing?

I lead, first one step, and then another. I
whisper what is for you to do, one choice, and then
another.

Often, there is waiting . . . and listening . . .
and trusting. Often, there is stepping out . . .
believing . . . risking. Often, there is looking for my
presence in the things you do.

Wait on Me, and listen, and take a step.
Look for Me in the moments. These decisions are
not too heavy for you to handle; these decisions are
not meant to weigh you down. These decisions are
not to fill you with worry about messing up and not
getting it all right.

Remember how we talked about rhythm, the
rhythm of walking with Me, listening for Me,
looking for Me? It is the dance. Remember how I ask
you to dance? You take a step, following my lead,
feeling my arms around you, my gentle pressure to
come forward, then step back, then turn, all the

while your hand is in mine and I know the way the dance unfolds, and I know how beautiful you look when you dance with Me. This is the best rhythm for you, the one where you can look into my eyes and trust my feet and the subtle movements of my steps prompting you to go here, then here. This is beauty: your stepping where I step, your trusting I know your way. You don't need to know all the details for the dance to be beautiful and be perfectly right.

Your hands fit perfectly here, the way your fingers curve around mine. Your arms fit perfectly here, the way they reach up and out, bent and strong. Your feet know the steps I teach you. Keep stepping out, ready for pauses, alert and ready for subtle changes in pace, in movement. I love how you do this, daughter. This is a dance all our own.

Know How You Know?

So faith comes from hearing, and hearing
through the word of Christ— Romans 10:17

REMEMBER WHERE I've been, my child.
Remember how I've held you, how I've walked with
you, how I've always been near. I know you struggle
here. I know you wonder, "Have you? Have you been
close to me, God? Have you been near? I am hurting.
I don't know the way to You. You don't feel close.
What does it mean to live with You close?"

Look deep within you first. Sit in a quiet place where you can be still, if only for a few moments. There is my word to read, the way this world began, the lives I've loved, the stories of adventures and glory and stumbling and pain. Stories of falling and getting up again and choosing to believe in something more than yourself for strength, for hope, for a future. And these are more than stories.

But, also, there is a listening I want to teach you, a discovery of who you are with Me, unique from everyone else. I have placed within you the map to find Me, your heart yearning for more than what you physically see. I show you beauty around you, hope and possibility in the smallest, most hidden places. But to see with my eyes, there is a listening that comes from within your heart, the place where we connect, the place where I speak to you.

Do you know how you are familiar with the voice of your closest friends? Do you know how you are so familiar you can sense their presence in a room without looking up? You know the sound of their step, their shuffle, the slide of their foot, the way the floor creaks when they pivot and stand. You know their voice, the subtle variations as they speak, revealing their mood, the expression of their heart.

You know, without having to look at them, exactly their mood—if there is laughter in their eyes, or sorrow, tears beginning to spill. You know how their voice cracks when they are nervous and how their laughter starts small at first and then grows, to fill a room. You know your friends' pasts, their stories, their pain, their glories, what has made their hearts ache, what has made them smile.

And how do you know all these things? How do you know these voices, these hearts? How are you so familiar with one another?

You have listened. You have watched. You have been vulnerable. You have spent time together. You have been present with one another when the waves have swept high and times have been difficult and long. You have been present with one another when the sun shines warm on your faces, and laughter comes fast and easy.

Come to Me, daughter. Sit with Me. Become familiar with Me. Spend time with Me. Let Me teach you the sound of my voice in you. Listen close now. Let Me show you what makes Me smile, what makes Me sad. I know you. *I know you.* So come be with Me. I invite you to know Me, too.

The One Thing I Ask
You to Do

Therefore, we are ambassadors for Christ,
God making his appeal through us. We
implore you on behalf of Christ, be reconciled
to God — 2 Corinthians 5: 20

YOU CAN BELIEVE you're alone. You can believe
you're no good. You can believe you've gone too far.
You can believe your mistake can't be fixed. I know.

You can believe you don't deserve to be
loved. You can believe there is no way out. You can

209

believe your life is one of destruction and problems and this last thing you did, well, it just can't be turned around.

You can believe you're trapped. You can believe you're worthless. You can believe you're doomed and unlovable and not desired. I know.

You can believe all these things. Yes. Or, you can declare your inheritance, a seemingly impossible, completely true inheritance. You can claim your voice, your future, the gift of knowing there is always another way; there is always hope; there is always a path through the seemingly impossible. For *I* am possible. You are not possible. No, not alone. But I am here. I am here. And *I* am possible.

I am the way. Never you. *Never try to make your own way.* That is how you lose your way. You are not lost, now, when you cling to Me. You are not lost when you remember you are found. *You are found.*

You are found by the One who adores you and waits for you and celebrates with wild abandonment when his daughter is found.

Choose the life of knowing you are not lost, not one little bit, but found. And when mistakes are made you wish you could take back, don't try to figure out a solution by yourself. Remember, you are not the way. I have come. I lead. I am the one with the plan.

And do you know what the plan always involves? Do you know—no matter what has happened, no matter what you've said or done—the one thing I always ask you to do, the one thing my plan always involves?

Love.

You Need a Friend

We used to take sweet counsel together;
within God's house we walked in the throng
— Psalm 55:14

YOU ARE THE ONE I came for. You are the one
who makes Me smile. When you breathed your first
breath I leaned close, my spirit filling the room. I
want to be close to you. I like being close.

I remember walking in the garden, my arms
around my beloveds, the sound of their feet as their
soles touched the earth. I remember their voices,

212

their laughter, how easy it was for them to walk side by side, share with Me their every thought.

They were good at intimacy because it was how I made them to be. They were good at vulnerability because they didn't yet believe there was anything to hide. I remember the coolness of the night air and the moment they knew I was walking in the garden yet didn't want to come join Me. I remember their faces, the turn of her head, the downcast eyes. *My daughter, my daughter, what have you done?*

You are meant to be with Me, my chosen one. You are meant to be with Me, walking in the garden. You are meant to be in community with Me. You are meant to be strong only in my presence, in the walks we do, always, in the garden.

This garden where we walk is everywhere I am, with you. It is the cool night on skin longing to be refreshed. It is the safe place where community lives and adventure begins.

Let Me walk with you. Let Me be your friend. And when we walk, look for the people who want to join us. It is good to surround yourself with friends who know Me. It is good to have a friend you can touch, walk with, in the garden—a friend who recognizes my voice. It is good to sit in a room with sisters and bravely not hide. I have made you to be bold, to live out who you really are.

You are capable of going where I ask you to go. You are capable of completing the task ahead of you. You are capable of hearing my voice. You are capable of stopping and resting and trusting. You are capable of surrendering, obeying, abiding, loving. You are capable of walking, in the garden, with Me.

What is getting in the way of believing you are capable? Are you letting the friends around you help you believe you are capable of walking with Me? Look for the friends I give you. Look for the community around you. Look for encouragement and find strength in my words, my story written out for you. Don't hide your true self, the beauty I've put in you when you were first designed. Walk freely, walk confidently, walk in community, my arm around you, with sisters and brothers, too.

We can all go together, deeper into the garden, deeper into the hope I have for you. You are not designed to be alone. Let's go together, seeking these friends, shall we?

To Be Set Free

For by grace you have been saved through faith. And this is not your own doing; it is the gift of God, not a result of works, so that no one may boast — Ephesians 2:8-9

I WANT YOU TO KNOW who you are. I want you to come to Me, head up, not down, looking sure into my eyes. I want you to stand, not cower. I want you to believe—and when I say *believe*, I mean, live out—the truth, *the truth of you* I see.

The truth of you cannot be articulated in just words. The truth of you is a name and not a name. The truth of you is more than a description of personality, a page of characteristics, a list of mannerisms and popular expressions.

There's something you must remember: You must live *your* truth. You must live, with determination and might, *your* truth. You must know who you are designed to be . . . if you want freedom, if you want liberation from lies, if you want joy.

You, my daughter, are mortal, yes. You are human and frail, and you can feel unimportant and small. You can feel vulnerable and unsure. You desire confidence. You wonder if you have what it takes to live out the identity I have created, specifically for you. You can agree with the enemy that you are not good enough.

But here's what I want to tell you: You, my daughter, are made to be strong, with Me. You, my daughter, are made to do things I've prepared, just for you. You, my daughter, are made to go forward, not back. And to go forward, you must fight and break the agreements you've made with the enemy. You must know I have come to claim you, the daughter I made. You must know your life has been paid for. You must know you are free.

And sometimes, with my truth in your heart, you must reject lies about who I am. You must do this. Don't wait. Do it right now. This it what it means to fight—fighting for freedom from lies. It is rejecting lies and surrendering to Me. It is fighting for your identity, the one the prince of this world wants to take from you.

So, when you are weary, when the world presses in, remember I am here with you. Know I am the warrior who never sleeps. Know I rescue and ask you to trust Me more than anything else. That is how you fight. That is how you know who you are.

That is how you are set free.

Hold Out Your Hand

And now, O Lord, for what do I wait? My hope
is in you — Psalm 39:7

IT MIGHT BE TIME to let go. It might be time to
empty your hands. It might be time to stop grasping.

Open up your hands. There are things I
want to place in them. For I *do* want you to hold on
to *some* things.

I want you to hold on to hope. This day is
full of Me. There is beginning here. There are things
for which to be grateful.

I want you to hold on to love. What is more important than you, than your own pursuits? What is before you, who is before you? How can you enter into a situation with my love pouring out? How can you show her, show him, my face?

I want you to hold on to faith. You do not stay in the hard times forever. There is good coming. There is also beauty here, right now. Look for Me and you will find Me. Listen for Me and you will hear my voice, all around.

I want you to hold on to joy. Joy is for you. Joy is for you to feel. Joy is for you to wake up with and experience and demonstrate. Could you imagine practicing spreading joy? It is for you to know.

I want you to hold on to Me. I want you to treasure moments, and I want you to be present with Me. Look ahead, to the future, and ask for wisdom so I may teach you the way to go, whether to spend time here or there.

I want you to hold on to grace, the forgiveness and life I give you. I want you to remember how I came for you and come again. I want you to live in freedom, breathe deeply, rest in what I give.

I want you to hold on to my hand, in everything you do. I want you to hold on to my hope, my love, my faith, my joy, my grace.

I want you to hold in your heart the image of you I put before you, the daughter clinging to her Father's hand.

Your Wedding

And I saw the holy city, new Jerusalem,
coming down out of heaven from God,
prepared as a bride adorned for her husband
— Revelation 21:2

MY DAUGHTER, my delight, you don't need to
compare yourself to one single person. There is a
wedding coming, a wedding where you are dressed
completely, by my love. You are surrounded by my
love. You walk deeper in my love. You are the bride I
have chosen.

You are the one chosen to marry the Groom who has come and broken His body for you. The Groom who has broken his heart for you. Come and be ushered into the kingdom of celebration—a place of singing and rejoicing. Can you see Him waiting for you? Can you see him loving you so much that He died for you?

You, my daughter, are complete, in Me. You, my daughter, are the one who doesn't need to look different and act different or have more or less to be chosen, by Me. You are the one I have chosen. You are the one I want. I can't take my eyes off of you, my dearest.

So, you ask Me, how do I protect your heart? How do you live in this world, one of comparison and envy and slander and thievery? How do you protect yourself from comparison when that is the culture in which you live and the wedding is around the corner but not yet a date you can perceive? How do you await my coming again, my Son's rescuing you again, in a world of tearing each other down and of pain?

Oh, my dear, look to Me. The only way to protect yourself is to regularly look into my eyes, see Me looking at you, see Me desiring you, see Me writing your name upon my heart and feeling sorrow when you believe you are not good enough to be desired as much as her, or her, or him.

Look to Me. Look to the choice of my Son, as He kept His gaze on Me. He practiced looking on Me, listening for Me, being away with Me. He removed himself from the world while remaining in it, too. It is possible for you, to remain close to Me and observe this world and be my daughter who desires to join Me in loving this world, while not being eaten up by the evil of it, too.

Practice coming away with Me. Practice looking for Me. Practice recognizing my voice. Practice looking at this world through my eyes and seeing yourself the way I see you, with a name, and a purpose and a mission and a beauty all your own. There is no one person, not one daughter of mine, like you. Come closer now. My arms are wide open.

This Not-So-Ordinary Day

Behold, I am doing a new thing; now it springs forth, do you not perceive it? I will make a way in the wilderness and rivers in the desert — Isaiah 43:19

THIS DAY is not ordinary. This day may be one of quiet or chaos, challenge or rest. But no moment is ordinary. It may be familiar. It may be predictable. It may make you frustrated and angry, discouraged and sad. It may be one where you see hope, hope all around. It may be the day you see deeper, go further, pursue a new place you've never traveled before.

I hold you in what you see as ordinary. I look ahead and stay here with you, in this moment. *Let me unfold it for you.*

There is a point where you can no longer see. There is a point where there are obstacles and there is nothing to do but wait on Me, look to Me, desire for Me to take hold of all control and guide you. *Where I guide you, where I am with you, is not the place of ordinary.*

There are the regular tasks to get done, the job to do, the responsibilities to complete. It may involve doing the same thing day after day, for a while, and another while. *But still, where I am is not ordinary.*

Here—here I am, with you. The intake of your breath, the feel of your skin, the ideas taking place in your mind, the beat of your heart. You are a wonder, a beauty, and *this day*, with all I've made, can never be an ordinary day.

Let Me give you new eyes to see so you don't miss the possibilities around you that *I* see. Let Me give you new eyes to see so you don't get discouraged and mistake *wonder* for ordinary. Let me show you how what *you* think is mundane may be an opportunity to be with Me in a new way.

I am always new and always the same. *You can always count on Me.*

loop

But I never stop wanting you to see the hidden wonder in this not-so-ordinary day.

In the Waiting

By this you know the Spirit of God: every spirit that confesses that Jesus Christ has come in the flesh is from God, and every spirit that does not confess Jesus is not from God . . . Little children, you are from God and have overcome them, for he who is in you is greater than he who is in the world
— 1 John 4: 2-4

THERE IS a still, quiet place, a dark place where light shines through cracks until it is full on your face. I want you to go there. I want you to go, by yourself, where no one else is, and I want you to practice waiting on Me.

Waiting on Me is not a place of being alone—really. For I am always with you. Waiting on Me yields alignment with Me. It produces greater trust in my will, helping you believe it is okay for you to not see what is ahead so clearly. You know that I see, and you trust that it is okay for you to trust my sight, my heart, more than you trust yourself.

Cast aside the things that weigh you down, and I will give you a new heart, a new spirit. Cast aside the focus on needing to know the future and all it may bring, and I will show you more of my face, this moment. And you will hear my voice, ever more clearly.

My daughter, be careful of this world, so full of information and attempts to figure out all that humans don't understand. . . Don't worry now. Don't think of what you don't know. Think on whom you know, whom you trust, whom to run to with your questions and your worries and your plans for the future.

Yes, plan for the future. Yes, think on the things that will allow you to practice being with Me, becoming more accustomed to my presence with you. For with your life you are called to practice worshipping Me, with all that you do. Your heart transformation, the new spirit I give you, occurs only through Me.

Transformation happens through Me when you seek Me and you know that my plans, even though you don't know all that they are, are good: good plans for your heart and for your future.

Striving for Change

Do not be conformed to this world, but be transformed by the renewal of your mind, that by testing you may discern what is the will of God, what is good and acceptable and perfect — Romans 12:2

MY DAUGHTER, there is one thing I need to tell you. You need not strive. Working hard is good. Serving Me, with your life, with your heart, thinking of others more than yourself, is good. But doing these things, truly, authentically, comes from a heart transformed, a heart surrendered, not a heart that is striving.

You cannot change yourself, although I give you the mind and the will and the motivations to take actions necessary for a person to be changed. Your will and your mind and your determination are just a piece of what it means to be changed, for good.

It is a choice, a continual choice, of surrender, of deep-hearted commitment. Love causes turning in a heart–from the doing of one thing to the change needed for another. While your mind tries to get everything figured out, with a plan and a check-list and a way to measure yourself and your improvement, I look to your heart.

The day may not go the way you want it to, not according to your plan. The plan to do this or do that may not be accomplished. The desire to be measured by standards of this world may not be fulfilled. But daughter, I don't care about those things. I look to your heart. I care about the rich beauty held there, the depth of feeling and caring beyond yourself and your own desires, which only I can measure.

I have written you. I have created this heart of yours. I have created your mind and I know your personality, your will, the way you think about yourself, how you measure yourself, how you assess whether you rise or fall. And I have not made you to measure yourself. I have not made you to judge your worth. I have not made you to think so much about whether or not you are good or you are bad, you are successful or you have failed.

You are my girl. You are my daughter. You are the created one. You are created to point to Me, give honor to Me, worship Me. And because this is how you are made, this is what will bring you joy. This is the only thing that will end the striving, end the attempt to be a different person than whom I've created, so perfectly, so intently.

Trying to live your life in step with the rhythm of this world rather than the way I have made you will bring exhaustion, ultimately, to your heart. Let it sing and have room to breathe and be fulfilled! My love will fill you; it will fill your heart, if you want it to. So, put your hand upon your heart. Feel the beating rhythm I have created. It is rhythm of Home, of freedom, of rescue, of a life you were designed, by my breath, to live.

Let Me Come

And those who know your name put their
trust in you, for you, O Lord, have not
forsaken those who seek you — Psalm 9:10

MY DAUGHTER, I am holy. I make everything
holy. You have nothing to fear. I am bigger than
every thought, every ache, every fear. I stand before
you in the gap, between your belief and unbelief. I
stand before you—your God, your rescuer, your
redeemer. I stand before you and you are not
forgotten. You are held. Always.

233

If you want Me, if you want more of Me in your life, I will come. I will not hold back. If you want my love, if you desire more freedom and joy in your life, ask Me to come. Let Me come to the deep places, the dark places, the unknown places.

I know you. I know where in you I need to go. So trust Me. *Trust Me.* Let Me come. With Me I bring no fear. With Me I bring no sorrow. With Me I bring only hope and newness and life. I am life, for you, my love. With my love for you I bring life. I pursue you, and I will never let you go.

So, come. *Come.* Ask Me to come. Ask Me to enter in. You hear Me. I am close. *So close.* And I love you. You are the one I love.

Us Two and No Other

I am the Lord; that is my name; my glory I give to no other, nor my praise to carved idols — Isaiah 42:8

MY DAUGHTER, it is no mistake how I made you. It is no mistake the way you speak, the desires of your heart, the reason I call you what I do. To question the crafting of you is a question for Me, a question about my plan for you, a question about whether what is ahead for you is good and whether I can be trusted.

What do you hold on to other than Me? What is more solid than I am? What is more strong? What is more loving? What is more dependable? Do you know how I adore you? Do you know how much I love being near you? Do you know I love it when you pause, when you look up, looking for Me, and realize I am here?

For it is then that you allow me to hold you. You see my face and you behold glimpses of my glory and you want to stay with Me . . . And I hold you. I love when you pause and trust Me and want to be with Me and I get to hold you. It is just beautiful here, together, my daughter.

There will be a day when you behold me, full on. There will be no temptations to separate us. There will be no distractions by this world. But I will help you turn towards Me now, so you don't have to wait. It is best for you, for your heart, to not wait. I don't want you to miss what I have for you now. Not tomorrow, not a week or a year ahead. I want to give you the gift of my love right now. *Right now.*

It is so good to be together, to have you slow and feel my arms wrapped around your shoulders. There is a place where the two of us can go, and I want you to see it. It is the place where we go, just us two. It is your favorite place, the place of your every desire, your very heart's cry. And you're not alone there. I am with you. I am the only one who can satisfy these cries of your heart.

Will you let me? Will you let me now?

Move with Me Now

In him you also, when you heard the word of
truth, the gospel of your salvation, and
believed in him, were sealed with the
promised Holy Spirit, who is the guarantee of
our inheritance until we acquire possession of
it, to the praise of his glory
— Ephesians 1:13-14

I AM MOVING. I am moving in you and I won't
ever stop. You can't stop Me, and that's a promise
for you, my girl. I pursue you and I never tire and I
fight on behalf of your heart—your complete self—the

full you I created and have always designed you to
be. I'm not done with you yet, my darling.

Don't lose hope. Hang tightly to my
promises, the Word-come-down who breathes peace
to you and guides you along the rocky paths. *I have a
way for you.* I have a place for you to lay your head
and know you are seen and know you are wanted
and desired.

I have made you to be loved. I have made
you to give Me glory. I have made you to receive my
promises and my good plans—and to follow the path
so that others may see the path and have the hope
that is yours, too.

Behold Me, my love. Behold Me and never
be the same. Behold Me and stop making excuses for
not measuring up and being tired and waiting for
things to get better before you can surrender to Me
fully. What is the road map, my darling? What is the
road map to Me?

Simple. He is beautiful. And you know Him.
You know His name.

So watch how He moves. Heed the Spirit I
leave with you. Know you are never alone . . . For I
want you to live like you *know who I am.* And I want
you to live like you *know who you are.* And I want you
to live like you *know this life I've given you* is for the
purpose of you being blessed by my love.

My love is for you. I am for you. *Move with
Me now.* See Me moving and *move with Me now.*

loop

This is what you were meant, always, to do.

What I Want to Show You

For I know the plans I have for you, declares
the Lord, plans for welfare and not for evil, to
give you a future and a hope
— Jeremiah 29:11

DAUGHTER, you can listen for Me. You can seek
for Me. And you'll find Me, right here. *I am right
here.*

You can work hard to find Me, search pages
in your Bible, soak up my truth, study scripture and

memorize passages until you know them by heart.
But I want you to know *Me* by heart, my love. I want
you to know that the women and men in the Bible,
my daughters and sons, were my children whom I
loved and pursued and wanted to be with, just like I
do you.

They are not unfamiliar to you. Their stories,
their mistakes, their trials, are yours too. And that is
why I wrote them down. For I want you to see Me
and where I was and where I am and be encouraged.

But there are pages being written now, my
love, pages of story with you as the protagonist. You
are the center of the story I am writing with you.
And you get to decide, so much, of what happens.
You get to work with Me in the shaping of your
story, the rise and fall of the details of your life.

No, you don't have control over it all. No,
you can't change the setting sometimes, or the other
characters with whom you interact. For sometimes I
bring those people in and these events into your life,
for you to see Me more, love Me and pour Me out a
bit more. But you do choose how to enter into your
story, or how to dismiss opportunities I bring, reject
people you could love. You have a say in what you
do within the story. You have a say in whom you
love and whom you don't love, in where you go and
what you do with your time.

Oh, your story, my love . . . Do you see it
written out? Do you see my fingerprints upon the

page? I love looking at it, all the good that has
happened, all the places in you where I want to bring
hope, all the places in you that still need healing, still
need freedom. There are places in you where you
still need to see where I was, how I loved you in each
place of heartache, disappointment, and pain.

So, let Me show you the story of your life
through my eyes. I have some new things to show
you, some rises and falls you have not yet seen. And
it's good. I will show you the places where I come,
with my presence and my hope and my love, to make
it good.

How does this sound? Let's look, together, at
your story.

Let Me Tell You About Our Place

But God, being rich in mercy, because of the great love with which he loved us, even when we were dead in our trespasses, made us alive together with Christ – Ephesians 2:4-5

CAN I SHOW YOU where we can go together? Can I dance with you, grab hold of your hand, my fingers clasped around your palm? You are graceful when you dance with me. You are free, your steps light and sure. You plant each foot firmly into soil. You know this ground, this earth. The floor is level and you respond, fully, to my subtle hints at what will be the next move to make.

You trust Me. You know Me. You want to be with Me. You know who you are and your burden is light and your smile is radiant and your eyes shine. You are home. *You are home.*

You let Me take you deeper in, this place where the two of us can be together. And you follow Me, each move a response to my movement. You only lean when I lean. You only pivot when I turn. Your eyes are on Me and the whole world is here, *right here*, us two.

You know you are seen and wanted. You know you are made and chosen and breathtaking. I look at you, and I must catch my breath. I love to watch you. I love to be with you. I love to hold you in my arms and be your safe place and let you be quiet and let you be angry and let you be troubled. I love to soothe you. I love to comfort you. I love to tell you everything is going to be okay.

My darling, hide away with Me. Hide away and come out, further, into the light. Hide away and go out, into the places where I move, holding your hand, beckoning you toward Me. *Always toward Me.*

Where I go and you follow, you know the steps because I am just ahead. Keep your eyes on Me. Keep your hand pressed into mine, and you will hear only music, the music of laughter when you know joy, the music of tears when you cry, the music of whispers when your heart is troubled.

I stay with you, and I ask you to stay with Me. I am for you. I love you. This is our place. The place where you stay with Me and go where I go.

You're Not Made to Be Alone

We are to grow up in every way into him who
is the head, into Christ, from whom the whole
body, joined and held together by every joint
with which it is equipped, when each part is
working properly, makes the body grow so
that it builds itself up in love
— Ephesians 4:15-16

I CALL YOU BACK. I call you back, into my arms.
Don't doubt what I've made, how I've made you.

Stay close to Me. Hear my voice, where light falls in shadows, where noise rises and you aren't sure how you could ever truly hear Me. *You hear Me. I am near.*

My daughter, being with Me, hearing my voice, letting Me lead you, requires a turning over of your heart. You can't press in deeper by fighting to get to Me, by floundering desperate for Me. Rise up now and see where I am. Right here. *I am right here.*

No excuses now. You are designed for relationship, for relationship with Me. You are designed for community, for your heart to crave connection, people who know you and love you. You are designed to be known, understood. You are designed to be loved. *Loved.*

And I love you perfectly and completely. There is no other love you need to chase down. And I bring people into your life who are designed to love, too. And they are called to love you. And they are called to reflect Me to you. And they are called to help you hear Me. And they are called to help you walk straight where I walk straight, and turn when I turn.

You, my daughter, are not made to be alone. So if you are lonely and you are misunderstood and you are longing for an arm around you now, a friend to sit beside you, a person to experience your life with you, lift you up when you are weary and down . . . call on Me, my dear one. Call on your Father who made you, who designed you to yearn for connection. And then take a risk, into the adventure I call you to, and trust the safe places I've created for you, with others, to see Me and hear Me and lean on Me.

It's not better to be independent, solitary, all the time. Go away with Me, yes, but find Me, too, among the body, my home, my church. I will show you how to go forward. I will show you how to trust. I will protect your heart as you stay close to Me and take risks and head into what feels dangerous and unknown. This world is dangerous, and you have a helper. You have a helper in Me.

What You Might Take for Granted

Then the Lord God formed the man of dust from the ground and breathed into his nostrils the breath of life, and the man became a living creature — Genesis 2:7

MY DAUGHTER, listening to Me is a practice I want to teach you. So, first, take a deep breath. And again. Slow down now. Wait a bit, for Me. For I am here. Trust that I am here. As you listen to the sound of your breath, as you feel your lungs expand—

the air pushing through, your chest rising and
falling—think about inhaling Me, breathing Me in. I
am as close as your breath. I have created you so I am
in you, part of you. I am the natural rhythm of your
breathing.

Inhale. Breathe deeply now. Be aware of that
sound, the sound of your body inhaling. One breath,
and then another. Think of Me when you breathe. It
is something you take for granted, isn't it, this
breathing? You assume the air will be there for you
to breathe; your lungs will have what they need so
that you can live another day. Your body needs air,
but you need Me. Your soul needs Me more than
your body needs air.

I am what you are desperate for. You are not
alive without Me. Your soul does not breathe
without Me. I am fresh air in tired lungs that live to
expand and take in this fresh air I offer.

Oh, daughter, breathe Me in. *All the way
now.* Breathe Me in.

And this is the sound of my voice in you:
your breathing Me in and breathing Me out. It is so
simple. Your thinking of Me is your listening for Me,
hearing Me, knowing I am in you and I love you and
you crave Me more than anything.

There is no magic formula for listening to
Me well. There is no complicated list of suggestions
to follow. I have no check list. I have no program to
offer you. But I have myself to give you—to give you

again and again. And when I give you myself I give you all of myself. I don't hold myself back from you. I do not set myself apart. I want no separation from you. *I give you all of Me for I want all of you.*

So breathe, my child. Breathe Me in. *All of Me.* Think about how much you need Me . . . And my love for you will pour out, and you will know Me more, and my goodness will flood your heart. Then, you will know, even more, whose you are and who you love and how good it is to breathe air. Air that is pure, air that is fresh, air that sustains.

So You Want to Be Someone Different?

You shall have no other gods before me
— Exodus 20:3

LET'S DO SOMETHING different. Let's have you
pretend you are someone different, someone
completely different than whom I have made. You
can decide your appearance, your personality, your
strengths. You can decide your quirks, your special
hidden talents. You can decide what makes you
unique, valued, worthy. You can decide what it

253

means to be a woman I am delighted to look on and
call precious, adored, daughter.

Do you see her? Do you hear her? Can you
grasp the picture you've created, this imaginary girl
concocted in your head?

Is she all you want her to be? Don't leave
anything out. Write her out. Imagine her. Is she so
different from you? Is she like you or the opposite of
everything I've made you to be?

How is her worth measured? How did you
decide to write her eyes the way you did, or make her
laugh like that, or have her get things done so
quickly, so efficiently, so perfectly? Who is this girl-
woman you've created whom you worship and think
I love more than I could ever, possibly, love you?

Why do you worship this pretend self you
wish existed rather than Me?

She needs to be destroyed now, you know.
She needs to be thrown into the fire, where all lies
need to be sent to be destroyed, for good. This
imaginary girl you've created in your head is not the
daughter I have crafted with my two hands. She is
not the woman I have born with my breath and
designed, in all your wondrous and perfect beauty, to
be.

Throw down this lie you chase that makes
you strive towards imaginary perfection. You will not
receive my joy, my peace, my life in you that sustains
if you continue to chase what is not meant for you to

attain. Who are you to decide what it means to be
desired, perfected, worthy? Who are you to shun
what I've made and desire something different?

Let me show you this daughter of mine. Let
Me show you the beauty of her, the joy she brings
Me, the strength in her to love just the way I've made
her to love, to work with the passions I've given her
to use. She is mighty when she knows who and
whose she is and abandons all idols that bring
distraction to this life I've given her, distractions that
bring death to her heart.

For I bring life, my daughter. I bring you life.
And this life I bring you is in you. I am in you. You
are my delight and the one I sing over and never,
ever want to leave.

You Can Hear Me

Incline your ear, and come to me; hear, that your soul may live; and I will make with you an everlasting covenant, my steadfast, sure love for David — Isaiah 55:3

WALK SLOWLY and steadily, daughter. I'll let you know when the pace needs to be fast. Sometimes it does. Sometimes I move quickly with you. But it's a pace that's never hurried. It's okay to slow, for in the quiet you can hear Me more clearly. And then when you've spent time with Me there, and you know my voice there, you'll hear my voice in the rhythm of work, in the rhythm of serving. You can't do these things with Me without believing you hear Me.

In everything you do, you can listen for Me. It's not that I speak to you constantly, in words; but I am with you constantly. And my presence is the language of your heart you're created to hear.

Training yourself to notice how I'm with you is not for the purpose of following a rule. You are able to get through a day without Me—but not well. Just not very well. We are made to be together, the two of us. I'm never alone, and you're not made to be alone. Let's go together, shall we? Do you see how I hold out my hand?

Practicing seeing where I am is responding to my life in you. It's not turning Me away. It's realizing, a bit more, the fullness of who you are.

You see, *I see you.* I see the real you, the daughter in all her fullness, in all her completeness. I know where you're going. I know where you've been. I am with you now, seeing you here and seeing the full beauty of my glory in you. You are made for so much more than you will ever know—unless you trust Me more than yourself, unless you live knowing I am for you, with you, in all things.

Don't worry about what it looks like exactly, to spend time with Me. Don't try to figure out the right way to listen, the right way to heed my voice. *Start with knowing I am with you.* Let yourself relax and lean back into my arms. See my face. Hear the beat of my heart.

I am with you. *I am with you.* Enter each moment anticipating how you can be with Me.

And then, my voice? You'll be *living out* each word to you I say.

Do You Wonder about the Plan?

For my thoughts are not your thoughts,
neither are your ways my ways, declares the
Lord. For as the heavens are higher than the
earth, so are my ways higher than your ways
and my thoughts than your thoughts
— Isaiah 55:8-9

I KNOW YOU want to see what's ahead. I know it is
difficult to not know, to not know what is around
the corner. I know you wonder if I have a plan.

loop

My daughter, how could I not have a plan
for this world? How could I not have a plan for you?
Do you wonder now, what does it mean for Me to
have a plan? Does it mean Me knowing all the details
of a moment in the future? Does it mean Me having
designs stretched out for what's ahead, a purpose
considered, an arrangement in place?

What if I told you the plan I have for you is
not for you to worry about? What if I told you there
is only a small part you can understand of all the
things I know and the things I want you to know and
the things you just don't need to be concerned with?

Here is my plan: I have good for you. It is my
desire that you know Me, that you love Me, that you
follow Me, that you serve Me. It is my plan, it is my
desire, that you want to be with Me, that you want to
talk with Me, that you stay here, *in this moment* with
Me, and concern yourself with knowing Me now, *this
moment*, and not considering all the details about the
future that I know and you don't.

What do you want to know? What do you
want to know that you think I am holding out on
you?

Here is what you need to know: I love you,
and I never forget you. Your life is my
preoccupation. You are part of my plan for this
world, which I love and which I desire to heal and
bring to life and have know Me.

do you wonder about the plan?

I don't want this world to miss out on what
I've always had for it, as I hold out my hand.

When What You Believe is True, Isn't

Be sober-minded; be watchful. Your adversary the devil prowls around like a roaring lion, seeking someone to devour — 1 Peter 5:8

COME BACK TO ME. You don't have to feel far away. You don't have to believe you are disappointing Me.

There are whispers you hear that aren't from Me. There are whispers to lure you away, that want to pull you far from the place I have for you, the place I am with you, *right now*.

Listen close: You are with Me, my love, and when you hear whispers that say I am far away, that say you aren't measuring up, ask Me what *I* think before you believe them. I'm never going to ignore you when you come to Me with a heart fully open. I'm never going to turn you away, and I love it when you trust Me with your every thought.

Let Me hold your thoughts, your dreams, your fears. Let Me contain them, gather them up with my hands so you don't feel crushed by their weight.

I place my hand upon your heart, the beating of your mortal body, while your soul, your spirit, is connected with Me. You are *here* and you are *there*—your body breathing air I breathed while I walked *there*, your soul breathing in my spirit as you walk *here*, with Me. For *here*, you sit next to Me, claiming your place among the saints and lifting your voice and soul in praise.

My daughter, I wrap you up in my truth, and you are free. Choose my truth over whispers that call you away and you will stay in my peace. You will stay and know my voice more deeply. For I have given you everything you need to discern the false from truth.

And pray for more truth to fill your heart. My truth is your battle armor: my community helps

loop

you hear Me and know Me; my words steer you and
feed you and lift you from darkness to light; my love
is not a distant, theoretical love, but a fierce, I-am-
here-and-I've-got-you love.

For I am love. *I am love.* Stay close to Me,
and the whispers will quiet. Stay close to Me, and I
will rise up for you. But to be rescued, I ask you to
believe in the rescuer. I am steadfast and present, my
darling.

Look up. Look up.

To Go Forward, It's Time to Go Back

Where shall I go from your Spirit? Or where shall I flee from your presence? If I ascend to heaven, you are there! If I make my bed in Sheol, you are there! If I take the wings of the morning and dwell in the uttermost parts of the sea, even there your hand shall lead me, and your right hand shall hold me
— Psalm 139: 7-10

OH, RESTLESS ONE, I bring you peace now. These years go by, and I stay. These images in your memory, pages you flip through from the past, I make them beautiful. I show you beauty, and I want to show you more.

You can't change the past, no. But you can look at it differently. You can't change those moments when you were little, when you were the little girl with the tender skin and pink lips you used to bite. You can't change that time, the one that hurts so much. Or, *that* one, the one you say you'd give anything to rewrite. *Oh, daughter, I want to show you what I see.*

So, while the past can't be rewritten, it can be made beautiful, even now, as you look back. I know what it means to not see one thing beautiful about a moment, to be filled with pain and sadness about circumstances. There are things that break my heart, too, you know.

But I forgive. And I will help you know how to forgive, too, as you look back at the pages of moments you wished you could change, the people involved. And yourself, my love. I need you to forgive yourself.

Let Me come for you like you need Me to. You can't even know how much you need Me until you get a taste of what I have to offer you: healing for your heart, a past washed white. *I make you clean, my daughter.* I bend low and wash you clean with my very hands, my heart beating for you, my love. My grace covers you. My love covers you. My life restores you and makes all that you carry so light, so light.

You are made to be free. You are made to see and live in the beauty of you I created. You are beauty because I made you, and you were not meant to live in fear and regret and sadness—especially about the past. Close the old book now. A new one is written for you. I have new pages to show you. The pages of your past are in this new book, with a fresh, clean cover, white pages, pressed new. *And then turn the page.*

There is so much more to write in this book, so many more stories and pictures to add. These pages are not flat; they are not one-dimensional. For you are in the story, my love. You are the story I am writing. You are the love I have made. You are the daughter who stirs my heart and who I have redeemed and who I show is worthy and beloved and whole.

So, grasp hold of my hand. For the new book to be presented to you, you need to let Me take you back to the places where you haven't let Me go with you before. You need to let Me show you the light in the dark places, the hope in the despair, the presence of Me in all the times you felt so hurt, so sad, so alone.

loop

And I will be holding your hand the whole time. *The whole time.* I promise.

The Best You I Ever Made

And I will put this third into the fire, and refine them as one refines silver, and test them as gold is tested. They will call upon my name, and I will answer them. I will say, 'They are my people'; and they will say, 'The Lord is my God'— Zechariah 13:9

I NEVER TIRE of being with you. I never wish I were somewhere else. I am here to lead you. I am here to shepherd you. You are in my care.

I care about every choice you make. I care about where you go and how you work and how you rest. I care about whom you spend time with and how you love. Yes, I care about that the most—how you love.

There is no measuring stick in how one loves. There is no way to compare, to say he does it this way and she does it that way. You are made to love uniquely, in the unique way I've made you to do it. You are whom I have made you to be when you love the way only you can. Your love makes me smile. And it is needed.

Your love—my love in you—is hope for people I love. It is kindness and compassion and gentleness and service. My love in you is what equips you to give freely and love without boundaries. Only when you love freely, with your personality and with your gifts, can my freedom be experienced in you. And that is what people find captivating.

Me in you? That is what is captivating. That is what shines. That is what brings people hope. That is what lets you care less about productivity and more about being with Me. When you are with Me, you are loving. And when you are loving, you are experiencing my freedom; you inhabit my space. It is what you have been designed to live. Joy. Freedom. Hope.

So don't second-guess how I've made you. I only made one you. Only one. You are the only one, my daughter. So inhabit my love and you will love in abundance without having to try. Because you will be being yourself. And, oh, that's just the best now, my darling.

How Joy is For You

As the Father has loved me, so have I loved you. Abide in my love. If you keep my commandments, you will abide in my love, just as I have kept my Father's commandments and abide in his love. These things I have spoken to you, that my joy may be in you, and that your joy may be full
— John 15:9-11

DO YOU KNOW I like to bring joy to your work?
Do you know there can be fun and light-heartedness

in what we do together? Do you know I am the one who invented music and laughter and dance?

Laughter, now that's something I love. And your smile—it doesn't have to be an outward smile; I know how you are made to smile, my love. You, my daughter, are made to have joy in this life. And it is here, for you. It feels like it is hiding, I know. It feels like it is difficult to attain—or, when you've attained it, it is fleeting.

But I am not fleeting. I am not leaving you. And consider this: If I am the only one who can bring you joy, if joy is the space I inhabit, if I am with you and my presence is with you always, then joy is with you, too. Want Me to help you to find it?

Take a deep breath now. Joy is being with Me. Nothing else. The practice for you is being with Me more often than you are. To find joy in what you do, you practice being with Me. And then, by being with Me, you make choices toward things I have prepared for you to do. You see what those things are, and you do them.

And even if the work I call you to do is difficult and challenging and stretches you beyond what you thought you could ever possibly do on your own, still, you are in my joy, for you are choosing Me in it; you are working alongside Me.

Here's how I bring joy to you: choosing to be with Me means you are choosing to surrender every other space that previously inhabited your heart. I want to inhabit you fully. You are made to be with Me, fully. Joy is only possible when the parts of you that you were unwilling to relinquish to Me are killed. The old self in you needs to die so the new self can breathe deeply in the new space with Me.

I create within you a new space, a new self, and that is where your joy is. And when you choose to be with Me you are rejecting the old self and letting the new self thrive. Your joy exists in the space where the two of us get to be together. And that place is within you, in your new self, and nowhere else.

You are made to be with Me, and anything that gets in the way of us being together is a choice you get to make. Let Me in, and I will take care of it. Let Me in, and I will clear away the dark places of the old self to let the new self breathe. I do the work once you choose Me.

So choose Me again. And choose joy again. Today, and then tomorrow, and also, when you lay your head down to sleep.

Choices

Trust in the Lord with all your heart, and do not lean on your own understanding. In all your ways acknowledge him, and he will make straight your paths — Proverbs 3:5-6

REMEMBER THE RHYTHM of being with Me. Remember the rhythm of rest as well as work. I've said this before: I am with you now, but living this life purely, resolutely, does take effort. It takes commitment and focus and resolve to stand fast with Me. It takes a heart stripped away of all burdens, all distractions. Everything in this world attempts to distract you from Me. But I give you what you need so you can do the things I've prepared for you to do.

275

But you have to believe Me. And you have to live believing Me, with every action you take.

But maybe I am not what you are pursuing. What is it you are pursuing? What is it you are chasing? What is it you desire? What is it you spend most of your days thinking about, longing for? What is it you worry about, wonder about? What are you working toward, leaning toward? What do you hope to accomplish? What do you hope, more than anything, this life brings you?

Be intentional, my love, about the choices you make. You are designed to make choices alongside Me, with my guidance, so you are never alone. But the times you do feel alone are opportunities to probe your heart, considering what drives it, what consumes it, what drains it. You are meant to have a pure heart, and anything in it distracting you from living purely, with intention and good purpose toward my good plans for you, needs to be laid down. Give Me your heart again, my love. Don't wrestle with that burden on your own.

So ask for more faith, and I will give it. So ask for more courage, and you will feel Me close. But that isn't enough. Try it out now, the faith and courage I give you. Try out the presence of Me within you being enough for you, and do the things I've created you to do. I will purify your heart. I will keep you and strengthen you and carry you.

choices

But you won't know I'm doing this unless you take some risks, trusting Me more than anything, anything, else.

Your Longing, My Desire

My soul longs, yes, faints for the courts of the Lord; my heart and flesh sing for joy to the living God — Psalm 84:2

YOU, MY DAUGHTER, are precious to Me. You, my daughter, are right in your longing. I love how you long. I love how you long for more of Me. There is so much more for you. There is so much more I have for you—and you discover the desires of your heart when you listen to your longing.

278

All longing is born from a heart unsatisfied. You can be satisfied in my love and yet you are unsatisfied, as you wonder how you can be with Me in this moment, right now. You wonder how I tell you there is no separation between us, how I am with you always, until the end of the age, and yet, still, I feel so far away.

Why, God, you ask, do you feel so far away? Why can't I see you? Why can't I feel you? I hear about your arms being around me. I hear about you coming for me, desiring to heal me, how you speak to me and how you reach out and touch this weary heart of mine. And yet, I wonder, really, if you are here, for me. God, are you really there?

Oh, daughter, I hear you. *I hear you.* My daughter, I hear your cries in the night, the weariness and the frustration. I hear your joy when it comes, as well as the yells of exasperation and the cries of desperation and pain. Oh, daughter, *I know.*

I know it hurts sometimes, and I can tell you this: you have to trust Me more than the realities of the world in which you live. What you see all around you is not always the truth; it is not always what you should see.

My truth and the lies of this world will never match up. It is my desire that my truth penetrates this world. It is my desire that you take my words and you carry them in your heart so that your eyes see Me in this world, and your ears hear Me in it.

I desire you take my love for you and feel this world with my hands. I desire you let your feet travel where my feet lead you—my words to you, my love for you, guiding you. I will never ask you to go where I am not leading you first. Even in the places where it feels you are alone . . . if I am leading you there, I am there. I am with you. *I am with you, my child.*

So pray for my eyes to be your eyes. Pray for my ears to be your ears. Pray for my hands to be your hands. Pray for my feet to be your feet. Pray for my heart to be your heart. Yes, that is my desire: let my heart be your heart.

I have come for you, my daughter. My heart beats for you. Let the reality of my heart beating for you protect your heart and increase your longing for Me.

Let Me Tell You About Beginnings

And I saw the holy city, new Jerusalem,
coming down out of heaven from God,
prepared as a bride adorned for her husband
— Revelation 21:2

I LOVE BEGINNINGS. I love surprises. I love hope.
I love family. I love children. I love *my* children. I
love the stories of my family, all my children, and
how each moment is another day of beginning. It is
another birth, another white page.

281

And in the beginning there was no color, and I added color. And in the beginning there was no texture, and I added texture. And in the color and in the texture I added layers upon layers of beginning. All new. Everything, my daughter, is all new, with Me.

There is an order unfolding in a beginning. There is a plan shaping, one decision at a time. And while I have a plan and I know what's ahead, the discovery of watching *you* begin again never stops stirring my heart. For you are new, this day, with a story you've lived already, but yet still—*still, my dear*—brand new.

We've talked together now, about weddings. I've shared with you a glimpse of your wedding, the preparations I am making now for that celebration of beginnings to take place. I love celebrating my union with you. I love the celebration of the body fully formed, the bride united and whole.

Do not be dismayed by how things seem like they change so very slowly—how the difficult circumstances you face don't seem to go away. This temporary life now is a thin mask for what is still to come. Your yearning for Me—for connection with Me—ushers in the next beginning, you seeing Me in the midst of this world's worries.

I love the story of this world, and I love the story of you. I love the wedding for which you are being prepared. And I love how you get a glimpse, now, of the beauty of the wedding day and how it is the ultimate beginning.

Beginning happened the day the light was formed, the day my Son was born, the day the Word came down. Beginning happened the day all story began to be told.

Beginning happened before you took in your first breath, before your lips shaped into a smile. Beginning happened before the pain came in, before the regret shaped you, before sin was taken off your shoulders. Beginning happened when my Son chose to die so He could marry you.

Beginning happened the day He rose. Beginning happened the day you opened your eyes this day. Beginning happened the moment you sought Me, the moment of the wedding, the moment you trusted Me, and the moment you loved Me, and when you donned your wedding dress and you saw Me and you joined your sisters and brothers—like I ask you to now—to be with Me and call out to Me and be the wedding song I've made you to sing. This is the celebration. This is the beginning.

I am the beginning. Stay close, my daughter. I am where beginnings happen. Here, now, the moment you breathed your first and last breath.

Expect Me to Show Up ✍

My presence will go with you, and I will give you rest — Exodus 33:14

MY DAUGHTER, there you are. Step towards Me, and you will find Me. I do not waver in my affection towards you. I delight in being with you.

Cling to Me, morning and night. Step towards Me throughout the day. I am not silent towards you. But step towards Me. Relax against Me.

Slow to hear Me. Desire Me. I give you rest here, so adventure and faith will come.

First, Me. Nothing else. For I stir your heart in secret places, and I show you what I mean: You are not lost. You are not overwhelmed. The night comes and you know the way through, for you know where light is. You know where I am.

I bring light, child, and I am with you. I bring compassion, child, for I know what you need. I bring fresh air to breath and a new place to stand. I water the dry places, and the thirsty land is no longer parched, dusty, desperate for rain.

You lay wanting. You lay waiting. You lay down, weary to stand. But I bring you rest, shading you from intense heat. And I help you to rise, the strength of oaks whose roots reach down hundreds of years. I am more steadfast than that.

So, come to Me and rest with Me and lean on Me and you will be nourished and strengthened and hope-filled. Come with expectation of my presence. Yes, expect Me. Step out. Know that I am here.

Acknowledgments

To my God, my Father, the one who rescues and
redeems all that is broken, all that is lost. It feels
both strange and perfect to say thank you to you
here, at the end of this book. You are the reason
these words here exist. You have gone before me,
clearing my path, encouraging me to trust your voice
in me. You have shown me your delight when I've
tried to trust you more than any outcome or goal
attained.

So I give you back these words. I give you
back the prayers that underlie these words. I give you
back the dream that *Loop* will bring daughters deeper

287

into your arms, that they will hear your voice and desire to seek you more earnestly.

You are the one worthy of praise. Thank you for holding your daughters close. Thank you that you are here. Thank you for your words and your plan. You are so good.

About the Author

JENNIFER J. CAMP grew up in the middle of an almond orchard in Northern California. She was a small town girl who thought she wasn't good enough but who wanted everyone else to think that she was. The story she now loves to tell? It's the story of a lost girl and an almond tree and a gentle Savior who loves fierce. It's the story of a Savior who goes before us, wanting each of his daughters to know who she is, in Christ, and whose voice she is made to sing.

A former high school English teacher, Jennifer loves to encourage people to seek and live out the truth of their story, their identity in Christ. Jennifer earned a teaching credential from UC Berkeley and a MA degree in English Education from Columbia University, Teacher's College, after graduating with a BA in English, at UCLA. Jennifer and her husband, Justin Camp, are the co-founders of Gather Ministries, (gatherministries.com) a non-profit organization committed to bringing the genius of Jesus to the lives of busy women and men—women and men whose lives are filled but not full.

Jennifer spends her days trying to listen close to God's whispers, writing at her blog, youaremygirls.com, to encourage women to remember the truth of their identities, in Christ. She also writes with her husband, Justin, about the holy and hot mess of marriage, at holyentanglement.com. She lives in the San Francisco Bay Area with Justin and their three awesome kids and would love to connect with you.

Twitter: jenniferjcamp
Facebook: www.facebook.com/GatherMinistries
Blogs: youaremygirls.com | holyentanglement.com
Website: gatherministries.com

CPSIA information can be obtained at www.ICGtesting.com
Printed in the USA
BVOW04*1833061214

377973BV00006B/8/P